Getting Out from Going Under

Daily Reader for Compulsive
Debtors and Spenders

By Susan B.

Copyright © 2015 by
Getting Out from Going Under Publishing

All rights reserved. This book or any portion thereof may not be reproduced or used in any manner whatsoever without the express written permission of the publisher except for the use of brief quotations in a book review.

The excerpts from the Big Book, Alcoholics Anonymous are reprinted with permission of Alcoholics Anonymous World Services, Inc. ("A.A.W.S.") Permission to reprint these excerpts does not mean that A.A.W.S. has reviewed or approved the contents of this publication, or that A.A.W.S. necessarily agrees with the views expressed herein.

First Printing, 2015

Published by:
Getting Out from Going Under Publishing

ISBN 1-4818141-6-8

More by Susan B.

GettingOutfromGoingUnder.com blog
FearlessBudgeting.com Free Training for
Compulsive Spenders
ICantStopSpending.com Podcast
HealingDoodle.com Art & More

Dedication and Acknowledgements

This book is dedicated to the still suffering compulsive debtor and spender.

Thank you to Debtors Anonymous for saving my life one day at a time.

I also want to thank two other recovering debtors and spenders who were integral in making this book happen. They have asked to remain anonymous, so I will respect that, but I must thank them for the amazing support and feedback they offered throughout this process.

To my husband Jay, I owe enormous thanks for his unending support during the writing of this book.

My appreciation goes out to the Merriam-Webster Online Dictionary for the definitions used in this book and for helping me find words and synonyms when my brain couldn't.
www.merriam-webster.com

And finally, thank you to Kit Foster and his assistant Robert Chute for a fabulous book cover.

Table of Contents

Dedication and Acknowledgements
Please Read
Are We Abstinent or Solvent?
Helpful Information
January 1: Resolutions
January 2: Debtor vs. Spender
January 3: Comfort Is Overrated
January 4: Elastic Assistance
January 5: The First "Bite"
January 6: Budgets Are Like Diets
January 7: Winning the Lottery
January 8: The Ultimate Ahhhh
January 9: A Newfound Hope
January 10: Pain vs. Misery
January 11: Savings Categories
January 12: Clarity
January 13: Spending Plan Vagueness
January 14: There Is Always a Choice
January 15: A Spiritual Cure
January 16: Vagueness Around Our Debt
January 17: Do You Qualify?
January 18: Brambles and Recovery
January 19: Honesty
January 20: Open-mindedness
January 21: Willingness
January 22: A Lifeline
January 23: Pressure Relief Groups
January 24: Giving In, Giving Up
January 25: The Bottom Line
January 26: A Prayer for Gratitude
January 27: Compulsive Spenders
January 28: Bank Reconciliation

January 29: It's Physical
January 30: Myths vs. Miracles
January 31: Stepping into Honesty
February 1: Program Glue
February 2: Gray Is the Color of Recovery
February 3: Romancing the Drug
February 4: Faith vs. Belief
February 5: It Works If You Work it
February 6: Why Am I Here?
February 7: Going to Any Length
February 8: What Kind of Recovery Do I Want?
February 9: Advice vs. ESH
February 10: Staying the Course
February 11: Going Through the Process
February 12: Sponsor Role
February 13: The Safety Net
February 14: Valentine's Day A Plea for Sanity
February 15: A Bridge Between
February 16: 10,000 Hours
February 17: Disappointment Is Not Fatal
February 18: Pick Your Pain
February 19: Making It Work
February 20: A Grateful Heart
February 21: Cost vs. Price
February 22: A Psychic Change
February 23: Delayed Gratification
February 24: Change of Speech
February 25: Lending Money
February 26: Accepting the Unacceptable
February 27: What You Cannot Change
February 28: Hope
February 29: The Fine Print
March 1: Diving into Recovery
March 2: Now
March 3: Peaceful Means
March 4: Vision or Self-Will
March 5: Dominoes

March 6: PRG Humility
March 7: Feelings Aren't Facts
March 8: Keeping Numbers as a Spiritual Path
March 9: Why Me?
March 10: Equanimity
March 11: Measures of Progress
March 12: Sales Mentality
March 13: Justice and Compassion
March 14: Recovering or Recovered?
March 15: Giving Away Our Power
March 16: Giving PRGs Gently
March 17: Sharing ESH Consciously
March 18: Recovery Blueprint
March 19: PRG Parameters
March 20: Jumping Off a Cliff
March 21: Communicating with Creditors
March 22: Resentments & Forgiveness
March 23: Fear Rules
March 24: Pink Clouds
March 25: Our Legacy
March 26: A Slight Nudge
March 27: A Matter of Perspective
March 28: Triggers
March 29: Why Is This Happening to Me?
March 30: The Glittering Prize
March 31: Faith
April 1: Lights, Camera, Action
April 2: Stall Tactics
April 3: Attitude
April 4: A Prosperous Life
April 5: Relief of Fear
April 6: The Second Arrow
April 7: Outreach Etiquette
April 8: Keep Moving
April 9: Gotta Have 'Em
April 10: Crucial 4Th Step Tips
April 11: Making Outreach Calls

April 12: Generosity, Not Grandiosity
April 13: Yes, Not Now, or Something Better
April 14: Accumulation
April 15: Income Tax Day
April 16: Don't Believe Everything You Think
April 17: Love and Fear
April 18: Deprivation or Justification
April 19: Living in the Next Month
April 20: Type A or Type B
April 21: Surrender
April 22: Embrace Your Spending Plan
April 23: Gift Giving
April 24: Vagueness Is Our Enemy
April 25: Dealing with Obsession
April 26: Feeling Our Pain
April 27: A Day Off
April 28: Sitting with Money
April 29: Analysis Paralysis
April 30: Self-Knowledge *Can* Avail Something
May 1: First of the Month Frenzy
May 2: Admitting to Our HP
May 3: Just Do It!
May 4: Intuition
May 5: Funding Our Contingency
May 6: Strong Sponsorship
May 7: Who Am I?
May 8: One Step Back
May 9: Customer Service
May 10: Deprivation Mentality
May 11: Good Decisions
May 12: Creditors Do Not Come First
May 13: Firm or Mean?
May 14: Family Support
May 15: Awareness vs. Planning
May 16: Fame Is Not a Feeling
May 17: Bigger Is Not Better
May 18: You ARE an Artist

May 19: Prosperity Isn't Always Cash
May 20: Having Money Before Spending It
May 21: Do What You Love and…
May 22: Gratitude Makes Acceptance Easier
May 23: Keep It Simple
May 24: Balance
May 25: Together
May 26: Financial Security
May 27: The Enemy of Creativity
May 28: Uselessness and Self-Pity
May 29: All in the Family
May 30: Saving the World
May 31: Integrity
June 1: Do Your Part
June 2: Tracking Sporadic Income
June 3: Live in Peace
June 4: Visions Cost Money to Fulfill
June 5: Enthusiasm
June 6: Finding Balance
June 7: Persistence, Not Perfection
June 8: Justifying Relapse
June 9: Merging Money
June 10: Hobby or Business?
June 11: Service at Meetings
June 12: Layaway
June 13: Communications Is Vital
June 14: Fellowship and Faith
June 15: Acceptance Is the Key
June 16: Progress, Not Perfection
June 17: Preference and Desire
June 18: Sometimes…
June 19: Facing Fear of Death
June 20: Patience as a Spiritual Practice
June 21: The Value of Silence
June 22: Hearing or Listening?
June 23: What Does Fame Feel Like?
June 24: Just Say No

June 25: Overwhelm
June 26: There Is Enough
June 27: The Future
June 28: Our Assets
June 29: Acceptance and Gratitude
June 30: Determined Effort
July 1: Removing Our Shortcomings
July 2: Slaves to Our Defects
July 3: Self-Care
July 4: Freedom
July 5: We are Not Our Debts
July 6: Do I Deserve That?
July 7: Talking to Kids About Money
July 8: Stand Strong
July 9: Fearing the Truth
July 10: The Spending Plan's Potential
July 11: Anger and Sadness
July 12: A New Way of Thinking
July 13: Partner Challenges
July 14: Slow and Steady Practice
July 15: Reflection
July 16: Relationship Anonymity
July 17: Action Plan
July 18: A Work in Progress
July 19: Taking Care of Business
July 20: Accumulated Funds
July 21: Saving for What We Want
July 22: Shifting My Thinking
July 23: Financial Choices
July 24: Self-Worth
July 25: Category Detail
July 26: Passing Moments
July 27: How to Apologize
July 28: Being Right or Being Happy
July 29: Fear of Creditors
July 30: The Race to Hit Bottom
July 31: Sisterly/Brother Love

August 1: Forgive and Forget
August 2: Jealousy and Envy
August 3: Regretting the Past
August 4: Dependence
August 5: Active Reflection
August 6: About Amends
August 7: Obsession's Fallout
August 8: Consequences and Forgiveness
August 9: All Are Welcome
August 10: Spending Moratorium
August 11: Right Action; Right Thinking
August 12: Rigor
August 13: Anonymity Prevents Gossip
August 14: Literature
August 15: Correcting Others
August 16: Writing
August 17: Positive Pitches
August 18: More
August 19: Boredom
August 20: Creative Outlets
August 21: I am Not My Money
August 22: Two Slogans for the Storm
August 23: Emotional Rollercoasters
August 24: Ask to See the Truth
August 25: Racing Thoughts
August 26: Fear vs. Commitment
August 27: Serenity Before Prosperity
August 28: It's Not Fair
August 29: Program Burnout
August 30: Giving Charity
August 31: Humility
September 1: Making Amends
September 2: Before We are Halfway Through
September 3: Peace & Serenity
September 4: Distraction
September 5: Opening the Envelope
September 6: Home Groups

September 7: Business Meetings
September 8: Courtesy
September 9: Budget vs. Spending Plan
September 10: Living Within Our Means
September 11: Conditional Recovery
September 12: Humility with Numbers
September 13: A Prayer for Remembrance
September 14: Seeing Clearly
September 15: The Last Thing to Go
September 16: Why Accrue?
September 17: Spiritual Practice Not Spending
September 18: Self-Delusion
September 19: Thinking Ahead
September 20: The Source of Our Abundance
September 21: Rewards
September 22: A Thousand Names
September 23: All Is Fundamentally Well
September 24: Time
September 25: Temptation
September 26: The Past Is a Dream
September 27: Less Is More
September 28: Wimpy's Hamburger
September 29: Relapse
September 30: Justice
October 1: Personal Inventory
October 2: Benefit to Others
October 3: An Allergy of the Body
October 4: Consistent Daily Practice
October 5: The Big Picture
October 6: Magical Thinking
October 7: Carrying the Message
October 8: Being Prepared
October 9: The Best
October 10: Finding Loopholes
October 11: Underearning
October 12: Insurance
October 13: Gambling

October 14: Hoarding
October 15: Why Do We Debt?
October 16: When Things Go Wrong
October 17: Change
October 18: Lack of Clarity
October 19: Spiritual Wealth
October 20: An Asset List
October 21: Taking Others' Inventory
October 22: If Only…
October 23: Disappointment
October 24: Getting Out of Your Head
October 25: Failure
October 26: Window Shopping
October 27: Beauty
October 28: Laughter
October 29: The Telephone
October 30: Enlightenment
October 31: Perseverance
November 1: Sought Conscious Contact
November 2: Simple Meditation
November 3: Daily Inventory
November 4: Grace
November 5: Inventory Checklist
November 6: Transferring Addictions
November 7: After the Storm
November 8: Pride or Gratitude
November 9: Slowly, But Surely
November 10: Clutter
November 11: Life's Small Tragedies
November 12: Service List
November 13: Defining Our Recovery
November 14: Courage
November 15: A Prayer for Hope
November 16: Grateful for Relapse
November 17: Slip or Relapse
November 18: Committing Our Spending
November 19: Spending Plan System

November 20: Consequences
November 21: The Power of No
November 22: Prepaid Credit Cards
November 23: Prison or Freedom
November 24: Thanksgiving Acrostic
November 25: Thanksgiving Gratitude
November 26: A New Way to Live
November 27: Practice
November 28: Fit Spiritual Condition
November 29: Weathering the Storm
November 30: Spirituality
December 1: Service
December 2: The Help We Need
December 3: Receiving Gifts
December 4: Life as Meditation
December 5: Credit Cards
December 6: Sponsorless
December 7: Solvency and Health Issues
December 8: Discipline
December 9: Solvency as Service
December 10: Selfishness
December 11: Sober in Business
December 12: Shame
December 13: Restraint
December 14: Avoiding Pain
December 15: Holiday Gift Pressure
December 16: The Mind
December 17: Self-Care Is Vital
December 18: Kindness and Compassion
December 19: Rounding
December 20: Primary Purpose
December 21: Vacation
December 22: Working the Steps
December 23: Half Measures
December 24: Breaking the Cycle
December 25: Benevolence
December 26: Pay It Forward

December 27: Comfort Spending
December 28: Retain, Return, or Regift?
December 29: Choices
December 30: Deposits and Withdrawals
December 31: Celebration
Resources
About the Author

Please Read

The "Getting Out from Going Under Daily Reader for Compulsive Debtors and Spenders" is not an official Debtors Anonymous publication nor is it endorsed by Debtors Anonymous.

This book was written by an individual who is recovering from compulsive debting and spending one day at a time, and wanted to share her experience, strength, and hope with others who are walking the path of recovery. The information in this book is strictly based on one person's opinion. This daily reader is also a guidebook offering practical tips and suggestions for working a program of recovery from compulsive debting and spending. D.A.'s *Primary Purpose Statement* says, in part, "We come together for one reason: because we are compulsive debtors …When we are willing to do anything not to debt, our underearning and compulsive spending habits are removed." However, the author has chosen to include compulsive spending in this daily reader based on her own experience. Anyone who suffers with compulsive debting (or spending) is urged to go to Debtors Anonymous to find meetings and support.

This book is presented with the heartfelt wish that others will be helped by it as they walk the path of recovery.

Are We Abstinent or Solvent?

There is an ongoing debate about whether those in recovery from compulsive debting and spending should call themselves solvent or abstinent. Abstinence is the practice of restraint. When we say we are abstinent in D.A., it means we do not indulge in behaviors that are detrimental to our recovery from compulsive debting and spending. D.A. members who call themselves solvent define solvency as the daily process of not incurring unsecured debt.

However, the literal definition of the word solvent is the "state of being able to pay our debts," according to the Merriam-Webster Online Dictionary. So the use of the term by those in D.A. really brings a new meaning to it, which is fine by me.

Does it really matter what word we use to describe our recovery? As it says in the Debtors Anonymous Preamble, "The only requirement for membership in Debtors Anonymous is a desire to stop incurring unsecured debt."

So in the end, it is our common goal of recovery that brings us together whatever term we use to describe ourselves. Because there is no D.A. consensus on which word to use, I have chosen to use the words "abstinent," "solvent," and "sober" interchangeably to describe the state of being in recovery from compulsive debting and spending one day at a time.

Helpful Information

The following acronyms and abbreviations are used throughout the book:

D.A.: Debtors Anonymous

BD.A.: Business Debtors Anonymous

PRG: Pressure Relief Group

ESH: Experience, strength, and hope

HP: Higher Power

Big Book: Big Book of Alcoholics Anonymous

12&12: A book called "The Twelve Steps and Twelve Traditions of Alcoholics Anonymous"

Book-end: Telling someone before and after you take a committed action

The Serenity Prayer
God/Higher Power, Grant me the serenity to accept the things I cannot change, courage to change the things I can, and wisdom to know the difference.

January 1 — Resolutions

Every day is New Year's Day for those in recovery from compulsive debting and spending. We do not make resolutions once a year on a whim and then forget about them. Each day we make a fresh commitment to refrain from acting out in our disease.

Just as important, we don't count on magical thinking to keep us sober with money. When we live by our spending plan and within our means no matter what, one day at a time (sometimes, one minute at a time) we are assured that we will never incur new unsecured debt again.

Some of us include committing our spending to a sponsor before doing so as further insurance against compulsive spending and debt relapse. The rest of the formula is simple, and clear instructions are laid out for us in the 12 steps. Daily admission of powerlessness over our disease, belief that a power greater than us can keep us sober with money, taking responsibility for our actions, working on our character defects, prayer, meditation, and service to others is our daily formula.

Just for today: Remember that our commitment to recovery is measured in days, not years.

January 2 — Debtor vs. Spender

Step 1 of Debtors Anonymous (D.A.) states that "we admitted we were powerless over debt ... that our lives had become unmanageable." Further, D.A. says the only requirement for membership is a desire to stop debting.

However, people have recovered in this program that came in with no debt at all! D.A. is a big tent and this program can apply to anyone whose life is unmanageable around money.

There are members of the Fellowship who had lots of money, but couldn't stop spending. Their lives were unmanageable; they weren't present for their family, and felt out of control.

There are others who recovered in this program whose problem was terror of not having enough and fear of spending any money, so they lived in severe and unnecessary deprivation. It is not required that you be even $1 in debt to qualify for this program.

So, please don't let the word *debt* deter you if that is not the problem as you see it. The key is whether your life is unmanageable due to money. Semantics are unimportant.

Just for Today: Remember that a compulsive spender is just a debtor who hasn't run out of money yet.

January 3   Comfort Is Overrated

The yearning for comfort gets me into trouble. I had to shift my thinking about this in order to stay abstinent with my spending. Staying sober with money and making good choices are often uncomfortable.

Many years ago, I went through a rough time of feeling restless, irritable, and discontented, and no matter how hard and how much I prayed for comfort and relief, I was still miserable. I was on the verge of losing my abstinence.

My sponsor, a lovely woman who suffered with many severe health issues gently told me that I should consider shifting my focus.

Instead of praying for relief, she said, pray as follows: God, grant me the strength to bear the discomfort until comfort comes.

When she said that, my whole world view changed. Now, when I say this prayer, I find that I am much comforted by knowing that I have not been given more than I can bear, and I can appreciate the reminder that all things pass.

Just for today: If you're suffering physical, mental or emotional pain, ask your Higher Power for the courage to stay sober with money until it passes.

January 4 — Elastic Assistance

The initial desire to spend may come out of nowhere, from a thought that pops into our head or something we see in a store window, TV commercial, or on the Internet ... but we don't have to add fuel to the fire by obsessing about the item.

When triggered, we have a choice. We can romance the obsession, a dangerous dance, or we can turn our mind to something or someone else

However, too often, the feelings cascade around us, and we are drowning before we know it, drowning in the desire, the flames of which we, ourselves, have fanned, and, if we reach the tipping point, we may give in to the obsession and lose our abstinence.

There is that moment between the first thought, which comes out of nowhere, and the next, which we generate. In that moment is the Grace of our Higher Power to make a different choice.

A program friend says she snaps a rubber band on her wrist as soon as the first wave comes, to break the pattern by allowing her to choose a different reaction.

Just for today: Try the elastic approach if you find yourself romancing the obsession to spend or debt.

January 5   The First "Bite"

For compulsive overeaters, if they never take the FIRST bite, they will never again have the binge. As compulsive debtors, if we never pick up the credit card, we will never debt again and if we live by our spending plan, we will not overspend again.

Whether it's a substance or behavior, we never again have to lose our recovery if we just don't take the first "bite." In D.A., we commit to not debting no matter what, and eliminate credit cards and all other sources of unsecured debt. Some of us further arm ourselves by committing every penny of spending before spending it. Even if we *want* to compulsively spend or debt, by taking these actions, we endure, and ensure that, just for today, we continue our solvency.

By doing our part, by just not taking one small "bite," we open the door for our Higher Power to remove the obsession, which is an infinitely bigger accomplishment. By not feeding the obsession and acting on it, we allow our Higher Power to give us Grace and pause, which is often all we need to be restored to sanity.

Just for Today: Ask your Higher Power to give you the willingness to do your part to keep from compulsive spending or debting.

January 6 — Budgets Are Like Diets

A budget is like a diet, something you go on and off, too often causing a binge in reaction to feeling deprived. In D.A., our spending plan is a life-preserver that can be molded as our needs change. We get help from others in the form of a PRG to develop and modify our spending plan so we can live within our means.

But as soon as possible, we allocate some money, even $1 a month, to self-care categories that the "budget" thinker might call luxuries, such as clothing, entertainment, and vacation. For us, these are all components of living in balance.

Yes, meeting our bottom line is the first step in physical recovery. We must learn to live within our means, which can be painful because it means saying no to instant gratification at times.

But after that, moving into more comfort is a worthy goal. With the help of your sponsor and PRG team, you can explore ideas for increasing income or adjusting your categories.

Just for Today: Remember that the D.A. way of life teaches us how to live in balance. Have faith that even if you only put $1/month in a self-care category, it will build up over time ... sometimes far faster than you think (D.A. miracles abound)!

January 7   Winning the Lottery

Let's face it, a lot of our "wants" are just for "stuff" that will satisfy us for a moment in time, only to be replaced by the next longing.

Last night, two tickets won the Powerball jackpot for nearly $600 million dollars. Naturally, I immediately began fantasizing what I might do with a few hundred million dollars.

Because money burns a hole in my pocket when my disease is left unchecked, I quickly realized that I might not buy Lear jets and yachts, but the nagging yearning for "stuff" would haunt me and I would not have a single night's peace until it was all gone. My life would become an endless pit of desire. As a bulk binger (I prefer a cart full of clothes at the thrift shop to one high-end garment), I'd be buying a never-ending stream of nickel and dime items.

It would be hell for me. Even accounting for charitable giving of 10, 20, or 50%, my itch would never be satisfied because I could never spend all that money down (like Sisyphus endlessly pushing the boulder up the hill only to have it roll down again).

Just for Today: Think about what has really satisfied you for the long term.

January 8 — The Ultimate Ahhhh

Today, I have a spending plan and every dollar is allocated to a category. Sometimes, it feels like a fortune in my categories, sometimes a paltry sum. But I no longer use up every waking minute planning how to spend a gross mountain of money, which would definitely make me miserable.

In recovery, we live by our spending plan, looking at our money in terms of categories, rather than focusing on the total amount of money in our checking account. In my case, that number is just a tool used by my disease to make me forget my needs when I get dazzled by my wants.

We can either be satisfied with what we have now, which takes care of our basic needs and often more, or believe the delusion that more would give us that ultimate "ahhhhh" of satisfaction, which we know is a lie, and living in that resentment of not having what we demand could lead us to relapse.

I have seen over and over that there is always a next item and a next item whether I gave in or not. I have never yet experienced that ultimate "ahhhhhhh" with any purchase.

Just for Today: Are you willing to work on your spending plan and assign all available funds to categories?

January 9 — A Newfound Hope

D.A. promises that "where once we felt despair, we will experience a new-found hope." By the time most of us get willing to work the D.A. program, our despair has infiltrated every part of our lives. We are hopeless, not just about getting out of debt or stopping the compulsive spending, but we see no way out of the black hole into which our addiction has tossed us regarding our relationships, work, in fact, our enjoyment of anything anymore.

For some of us, it takes quite a while to get to any sense of hope. We may be drowning in fear and panic. But eventually, everyone who works this program diligently experiences this "new-found hope." Even if your worst fears come true (e.g., foreclosure, losing a job), this program gives you tools to deal with any eventuality with grace and sobriety.

How can you not begin to feel hopeful as you learn to live within your means and stop debting? Even if you are not where you want to be, you have, at least, seen some improvement.

Just for Today: Despite setbacks, are you willing to stay abstinent and continue to work your program?

January 10 — Pain vs. Misery

I have had this expression pinned to my wall for years: "Pain is what I walk through; misery is what I sit in." There is a lot of angst in healing from our dysfunctional use of money. In the past, I gave in to the obsession to spend rather than walk through the discomfort. I never believed that it would end. But everything changes in life.

In my recovery experience, when I felt agony over wanting something so badly that I thought I would die if I didn't buy it, waiting was always the antidote. Every time I DIDN'T give in to the obsession, the obsession was eventually lifted. On the contrary, my addict mind lies to me and says that I will only feel better if I buy it, even if I can't afford it. The truth is that any time I do that, I always feel a rebound and want more. I never feel that ultimate "ahhhhhh" of satisfaction. Once I give in to buying when I am in obsession, I unleash craving and desire for more, whether I scratch any particular itch or not. There is a difference between buying something I truly want and buying something to (temporarily) stop the pain of obsession.

Just for Today: Remember that we can move through the pain of obsession without losing our solvency.

January 11 — Savings Categories

We keep categories to maintain clarity about our spending. For instance, we might have grocery, medical, entertainment, home, vehicle, bills, and debt repayment categories.

But we also create categories for accumulating savings for the future. A **prudent reserve** ideally contains six months of income for living expenses if we lose our job. A **contingency** is for current emergencies, such as an unexpected dental procedure when we don't have enough accumulated in our medical category. Many people aspire to fund this category with $1,000-$3,000. We also **save for retirement**, such as though a 401K through work. Finally, we can **save for special purchases**, such as for a new car, a house, or an elective medical procedure.

The miracle of D.A. recovery is that when we live within our means, we find that we are eventually able to set aside money for all these areas of our life. We may not be able to fund them at all initially, but gradually, we may be able to save $1 or more a month. This may seem too small to matter, but from this intention, many have been able to reap the rewards of having these backup resources.

Just for Today: Include savings categories in your spending plan

January 12 — Clarity

Vagueness deludes us with false reassurance and soothing denial. In D.A., our spending plan is the most vital tool for achieving clarity around our spending. What is the difference between having specific categories and just taking it from the pile of money that makes up our income? The difference is that we do our best to *plan* for spending in recovery. Vagueness leads to fear, anxiety, and panic, and to more vagueness which could lead us back to debting when we don't have enough left over for fixed expenses. But there are other ways in which we can gain clarity. For instance, if you are self-employed, ensure that you have a clear agreement on your fee before starting the work. Get clear on the cost of your doctor visit, lab test, specialist, etc. *before* you go. Find out all costs *before* hiring a handyman, landscaper, etc. If we prepare for spending, there will be fewer situations that take us by surprise and baffle us.

Just for Today, think about how you practice clarity in your program. If there is any area of vagueness, make an action plan to find out the information you need to become clear about it.

January 13 — Spending Plan Vagueness

Before we create a spending plan, it is suggested that we have 30 days' worth of spending written down, so we have some idea of what we spend in various categories. Even so, it takes a long time, maybe months or even a year or more, for our spending plan to feel like it's funded accurately. And most of us need an annual review because life's needs change.

Some categories have to be continually tweaked based on circumstances. For instance, properly funding the food category to ensure there is enough can be challenging, especially for those in a 12-step food program or those with children.

Pretending you need less in a category than you actually need in order to keep from living in deprivation can lead to resentment and, ultimately, acting out with money. Alternatively, over-funding a category can just be compulsive spending or hoarding in disguise.

Just for Today: Is your spending plan balanced?

January 14   There Is Always a Choice

Though we cannot necessarily stop the first thought about it, we always have two choices when we are drowning in desire for a purchase:

We can choose to romance the thought, spending our days on internet research to find the best deal, reading product reviews, exhausting ourselves by going to store after store to check out the product. Or, if we find a career training program if we want a new career, or new medical strategy if we are ill, obsessively posting questions, reading everything we can ad nauseam and fantasizing about it non-stop. All of this behavior will add to increased desire, which will lead to whipping ourselves up into an adrenaline frenzy, making abstinence from compulsive spending and debting far more difficult than it needs to be.

Or, we can recognize what is going on and pray for the willingness to stop. We can make a phone call for help. We can write about the feelings, not the purchase. We can stop the activity and do something else, so as not to further fuel the flames.

Just for Today: Give yourself a break from actively pursuing an obsession purchase until you no longer feel you will die if you don't have it or panicked that you will make the wrong decision about it.

January 15 — A Spiritual Cure

I will run out of savings before I run out of desires. It's not the purchase, but our attitude about it, that requires our effort. Obsession and craving are spiritual problems. We can use our program to find a daily spiritual cure.

We don't just want to be "dry drunks," hanging on by our fingernails. We are seeking recovery on all three levels, spiritual, physical, and emotional.

Learning this new way of attention to our purchases takes practice. No one said recovery is painless. They just say it is simple.

Just for today, if you feel gripped by a spending desire, recognize what you can do to calm the obsession, to let go, rather than give in. For today, don't fuel the flames of desire that are detrimental to your physical, emotional, or spiritual recovery.

January 16   Vagueness Around Our Debt

When we first come into program, we may have no idea how much we owe because we won't open the mail. But what do we do about it? Do we stay in the darkness or bring the issue into the light?

In recovery, we opt for clarity. Once you see the truth of your financial situation, you may cry, feel sick to your stomach, panic-stricken, horrified, ashamed, and/or humiliated. The truth may, in fact, BE your worst fears come to life, but pretending doesn't change facts.

When I became willing to face the pain of what I was using money to avoid, I became willing to put the drug down. Once we accept a life of clarity, we can start the business of healing and changing the things we can. We are then on the road to recovery, but now, we are no longer facing and dealing with the challenges alone.

Just for Today: Remember that no matter how bad things are, once you are willing to do what we have all done to get, and stay in, recovery, you will find lots of help and support. What you won't have are people to support your living in vagueness, because those of us walking the path ahead of you know the dangers of doing so, and prefer the pain we may face in reality to the torment of the not knowing, which brings only suffering.

January 17 — Do You Qualify?

With eating, drinking, or drugs, the first bite, drink, or hit is the bottom line, but with our issues, it's not so clear-cut. It took years for D.A.'s founders to determine that debting was the bottom line for membership in D.A..

But there are successfully recovering D.A. members who came in with no debt, but have other money issues. The fact is a compulsive spender is just a debtor who hasn't run out of money yet. And a money depriver is just a debtor who is filled with fear of letting go at all.

For some of us, debting is the end result of out of control spending or trying to fill a spiritual hole with stuff, a childlike inability to delay gratification, an addict's need for more, more, more. I have very rarely felt an urge to get a credit card or debt, but the compulsion to buy and spend is my donut, heroin, scotch and water.

Just for Today: Whether or not you have debt to repay, do you believe you are a compulsive debtor?

January 18 — Brambles and Recovery

I compare my abstinence and recovery in D.A. to the prince in Sleeping Beauty, slogging through the briars and brambles on the Recovery path. The sword is my spending plan, the cutting edge, the categories. Recovery is the princess.

My money is sliced up in a way that enables me to live without debting, to live within my means, ensuring both my needs and some of my wants are satisfied. Those brambles are the situations that confuse me, the obsessions that cross my path, and the temptations that could lead me back to debting.

Just for Today: Remember that you are the Prince in your own fairy tale.

January 19 — Honesty

Honesty is the cornerstone of successful recovery from compulsive debting and spending. Without self-honesty, you do not become willing to seek help nor even recognize you have a problem. Further, honesty prevents self-justification for actions that are counter-productive or will lead to relapse. They say self-knowledge may avail us nothing, but self-honesty, raw and deep, will lead us to a life of integrity and recovery.

Making a mistake is one thing, but lying to your sponsor about the mistake keeps you stuck in your illness. If you are determined to live a life based on honesty, you will invariably continue to be willing to tell the truth, even when it is painful or you risk losing your sponsor.

Just for Today: Know that being dishonest about your recovery is a sure path to relapse.

January 20 — Open-mindedness

Most people come into D.A. desperate for help. They have either hit bottom and lost everything or hit a higher bottom and there is still time to keep the boat afloat. Either way, only desperation leads us to a 12 step program.

Invariably, as soon as we are presented with D.A. "suggestions," we balk. Suddenly, once again, *we* know best how to recover from this disease. We may like this suggestion, but cannot possibly do that one. Even regarding the one point upon which all D.A. members agree, that we do not use unsecured debt, some may balk. When told that we accomplish this goal, first and foremost by cutting up our credit cards and canceling all lines of credit and loan accounts, who among us hasn't had a moment's pause? "But what if there is an emergency," cries one or "How will I rent a car to travel," moans another or "what if I need dental work," whines a third.

Just for Today: If you are only desperate and not open-minded, then you will revert to trying the easier, softer way again as soon as the feeling of desperation lifts. Just for today, remember what brought you into D.A..

January 21 — Willingness

If you are honest and open-minded, then you can become willing to do what is required for recovery, what has worked for others. Someone once said, "I don't have to like what I have to do ... I just have to do it anyway."

Willingness means we cut up our credit cards and cancel our loan accounts even if we are terrified about future need. We have faith that we will have enough and, if we don't, we will have help to address the situation. We can have this faith because we see that others have gone before us and succeeded. (More than a few of us nearly passed out from anxiety when we took this step.)

Willingness means not spending what you don't have available even if you want to cry and throw a tantrum. Willingness means giving all suggestions presented by your sponsor and trusted PRG team a try. Willingness to wait before a purchase allows urgency to die down.

Just for Today: Are you willing to do what it takes to stay in recovery?

January 22   A Lifeline

My spending plan is my lifeline. I don't live by my bank account, but by my categories. Living by my bank account for someone who burns through money like me, would destroy my recovery.

Instead, I assign every penny to a category, including savings and contingency. There is no slush fund or miscellaneous category as I cannot afford vagueness in my plan.

Categories accrue that are paid by a schedule, such as the annual pet license or car registration. I divide the total by 12 and allocate that portion of my income to the category each month, so when the bill is due, I have the total available, instead of scrambling to find the money all at once!

Discretionary categories accrue as well, so, for instance, if I choose not to buy any clothing this month, I have more money to use for clothing next month.

Without accruing in my categories and living by what I accumulate, there is no way I could keep track of spending in clarity. I would never be able to pay intermittent bills (like car insurance) and save for discretionary items without it. Living by my spending plan takes me out of vagueness.

For today: Review your spending plan to ensure it is working for you.

January 23 — Pressure Relief Groups

A pressure relief group (PRG) is a one to two hour meeting, either in person or on the phone, where two other D.A. members help us resolve financial pressures in our life, such as panic about debt, creditors destroying our peace of mind, having a crisis where we may lose our home, or having a medical emergency we didn't plan for.

Initially, though, we have a series of PRGs to help us set up a spending plan, without which we simply cannot work the D.A. program with clarity. Without setting up a spending plan with categories in which to allocate your money, how will we know that we have enough for our bills, much less food or other discretionary items? And without the help of a PRG team, we might make financial decisions based on self-will that are not in our best interest. Having two other people help us figure this out keeps us on the right track.

People also set up a PRG if they get a big financial windfall, such as a tax refund or inheritance. However, we can also have a PRG to help us figure out career decisions, family decisions, visions, etc. In the beginning of our recovery, many of us have PRGs monthly, or even more often if we are in crisis.

Just for Today: Is it time for you to have a PRG?

January 24 — Giving In, Giving Up

If we give in to obsession, we get to feel a short-lived "ahhhhh," or worse, disappointment in the purchase, followed almost immediately by another obsession hitting us even harder than the last, and less willingness to stay sober with money around it.

We then become severely restless, irritable, and discontented, and rationalize spending even if we don't have the money available. At that point, we will likely try to convince our PRG team and sponsor that we must take the money from other categories instead of saving for an item we cannot yet afford. Next, might come all out rebellion if we don't get our way.

When we begin to act out like that, the fire that began as a simmering flame now blazes out of control as we become less and less spiritually fit. So, which is the better choice: Temporary discomfort, followed by sanity and peace? Or temporary comfort, followed by hellfire and brimstone?

Just for Today: Think about which pain is worse in the long-run – giving in or waiting it out?

January 25   The Bottom Line

For new D.A. members who cannot pay their rent or afford enough food, the initial goal of this program is to find a way to earn or bring in enough money to take care of their basic needs. Paying down debt is always secondary to providing for our needs.

In D.A., we do not work for our creditors and we do not live in deprivation (which is not an excuse to go out and splurge!). We are striving to create a balanced financial life that includes debt repayment, but isn't driven by it. We ensure that, as soon as possible, we put money into categories for our pleasure (hobbies, vacations, clothing, etc.), and then begin repaying our creditors.

Knowing our "bottom line" is vital in developing a spending plan that allows us to live within our means. We don't have to feel embarrassed about our bottom line. What is important to me may be irrelevant to someone else. For instance, letting go of cable TV would really put me in deprivation as most of my entertainment comes from it; for others, cable TV is not at all important; and there are some who are perfectly happy having no TV at all!

Just for Today: Do I know my bottom line?

January 26   A Prayer for Gratitude

It is sometimes so hard for me to feel grateful when everything seems to be collapsing around me. I want to be grateful, but it is difficult when I don't feel that I have enough money and no solution seems to be forthcoming. It is challenging to be grateful when, despite my best efforts, my house is being foreclosed on or I lose my job or some other financial catastrophe strikes anyway. I forget to feel grateful when my relationships are in turmoil or my health is in crisis. Gratitude feels so far away when I am in the throes of desire for something I cannot afford and the thought comes in that I could buy it on credit.

Please, Higher Power, remind me to be grateful despite any setbacks in my life. Let me remember that a grateful heart doesn't binge. Help me to remember that there is always something for which I can be grateful despite the darkness that appears to descend. Let me remember that gratitude is my key to acceptance and recovery.

Just for Today: Please give me the willingness to have a grateful heart no matter what else is happening in my life.

January 27   Compulsive Spenders

Some compulsive spenders tend to get their high from coming home with shopping bags packed full of stuff, while others prefer to purchase just one or two high end items. But either way, the end result is the same. Our addiction forces us to engage in self-destructive behavior, spending beyond our means without any consideration of whether we can afford it. While the primary purpose of Debtors Anonymous is to refrain from debting, compulsive spenders will find relief from their addiction as well because the fact is that a compulsive spender is just a debtor who hasn't run out of money yet. In recovery, we create a spending plan that enables us to fund and purchase discretionary items in a sane and balanced way. But reducing the high we experience when we buy may take a long time. In the meantime, we must be patient with ourselves when any such lingering feelings are triggered. We may never completely eliminate the high we experience when we purchase, but if we engage in the spiritual program of recovery, we can reap the benefits of doing so because we are not letting our feelings dictate our actions.

Just for Today: Can you accept that feelings aren't facts?

January 28   Bank Reconciliation

Some D.A. members have never reconciled their income and spending with their bank account. They have a spending plan and a tool for tracking their money, but are vague about its accuracy. Unless you reconcile your actual spending with transactions in your bank account (and cash), there is room for a huge amount of error and vagueness.

Here are just a few examples of what might happen: You accidentally entered a transaction twice into your tracking tool without realizing it; a vendor incorrectly charged you (this happened to someone I know, where the debit slip said $22 and they charged him $220); you forgot to enter a transaction altogether in your tracking tool; there is an unknown charge in your checking account.

Lack of clarity about any of the above could cause you to overdraw your checking account. If the point of D.A. is not to debt and the path to staying out of debt includes clarity, then you can see how vital it is that you overcome your fear and learn how to reconcile your spending plan with your bank account.

Just for Today: Commit to reconciling at least monthly and more often, if possible.

January 29 — It's Physical

For many of us, the obsession is not about debting, but about purchasing. Some say they cannot relate to the Big Book regarding the physical concept of craving because we don't swallow money. It's true that we may not be ingesting a substance, like alcohol, sugar, or cocaine, but the adrenaline reaction set off by acting out with money *is* physical. Personally, compulsive spending and the aftermath of debting can make me high, breathless, lightheaded, angry, and panicked.

But if we don't give in to the obsession in our mind, we will never set in motion the craving that keeps it going. We can obsess about buying even a small item that we can't afford, to the exclusion of anything else. We can research it, ruminate on it, romanticize it, go to sleep with it as the last thought on our mind. That obsession can lead us into pain, deep pain. But the pain isn't bottomless … as long as we don't give into it. And using the tools of the D.A. program, we can help ourselves move past it abstinently.

Just for Today: Do you know that if you don't give in to craving, you will never fall into relapse?

January 30 — Myths vs. Miracles

There's a big difference between the miracles that occur as a result of working this program and the myth that money is magical and will expand at will. Examples of D.A. miracles are getting that job you wanted for more money because you became focused on your goal; accumulating the money to buy a car when you couldn't save enough to buy a cup of coffee before recovery; paying off the last of your unsecured debt.

Believing that money is magic and that once you are in recovery you should have unlimited funds in every category at all times to buy everything you want the very second you want it is a myth.

I was one of those people who thought that by becoming solvent in D.A. I would have no boundaries on my spending. Sure, I would be abstinent and wouldn't debt. But I assumed my reward would be to have more than enough money all the time, that D.A. was my genie in a bottle. The miracle I learned is that having boundaries around money was far more spiritually enlightening, fulfilling, and character-building than accumulating all the stuff I desire.

Just for Today: Do I want to live in fantasy or reality around money?

January 31 — Stepping into Honesty

The principle behind Step 1 is honesty. Without honesty, we live in denial about the fact that we are powerless over debting and/or compulsive spending, and continue to delude ourselves about the manageability of our lives.

Most of us come into D.A. because our behavior has finally caused such devastation in our lives that we can no longer lie to ourselves anymore. When we take this step, we soon become willing to stop lying to others as well. We learn how to deal with our creditors with integrity, instead of telling them what we think they want to hear.

There is tremendous relief in not living with the guilt of lying. Plus, when we are honest, we don't have to keep track of what we say to keep our stories straight.

Just for Today: When you become aware that you are about to manipulate the truth, remember this principle. Instead, take a chance on simply telling the truth.

February 1 — Program Glue

Step 2 of Debtors Anonymous states that we "came to believe that a Power greater than ourselves could restore us to sanity". Without the hope that we can recover from our disease, why would we go through this program and the major upheaval it causes in our lives and relationships?

This step gives us the reason to go on when the going gets tough and when our disease tries to convince us that our old, comfortable ways aren't so bad after all.

They say the further we are from our last binge, the closer we are to our next. So, no matter how much our disease tries to minimize our addiction, this step can be a constant, reassuring reminder that our old behavior was nothing short of insane and there is hope for recovery IF we relinquish control.

Just for Today: Remember that Step 2 is the glue we use to begin the process of reassembling our shattered lives after hitting our bottom and admitting complete powerlessness

February 2   Gray Is the Color of Recovery

Addicts tend to have black and white thinking. There is a right way and a wrong way ... and our way is the right way. In recovery, we cannot afford to think that way if we want peace of mind. That is why gray is the color of recovery.

A similar saying is, "You can be right, or you can be happy." Ah, wouldn't it be great if we could be both?! But more often than not, we have to pick. Of course, our addict self wants to be right.

But when I am even slightly spiritually fit, I know with absolute certainty that it is best keep my mouth shut when I feel that urge to prove I'm right. The feelings will pass. And when they do, I'll be happier in the end.

The same holds true with delayed gratification with our spending. When we are in that painful place where we want, want, want something and feel like we'll explode or die if we don't get it right then, it's really the same feeling we have when our partner, child, friend, co-worker does something "wrong" and we feel we MUST correct him or her.

Just for Today: Do not forget that it's not what happens to us that is the determining factor in our peace of mind, but how we react to it.

February 3   Romancing the Drug

In recovery, my sobriety and peace of mind are more important to me than the high I get from buying on sale. Unless I am planning a purchase, I delete sales announcements from my inbox without reading them. It's not always easy. At times, I've had to remove myself from the list completely because just seeing the email made me hyperventilate with desire. I know if I look at items on sale just for fun, I get a "contact high." It's not pleasant; it just fills me with desire.

This is where the spending plan comes in to provide essential support. If you live by your spending plan, you are limited to what you will spend in any category. So, sale or not, if you don't have the money, you will just cause yourself unnecessary pain by looking at the item, which may lead to resentment.

But, there is another danger. Even if you do have the money, if you find yourself getting high at the thought of the savings and embark on a spending binge, which may be abstinent, but may not be sober, how will you feel about it tomorrow?

Just for Today: Remember that our disease is cunning and baffling, and powerful. Could buying for the sale be a slippery slope that could lead to a slip or relapse down the road?

February 4 — Faith vs. Belief

When we become open to doing things another way, only then is there the possibility of being restored to sanity. The Big Book and the program of Debtors Anonymous have a complete plan to help us do just that. Whether you believe that power is the group or God doesn't matter. All Step 2 really asks is that you have faith that if others followed these steps and got better, then you can as well.

But before you can come to believe, you have to have faith. Faith is trusting that what has happened for others *can* happen to you. Belief is seeing it miracle happen in your own life.

Step 2 is about *coming to believe*. It is not a once-and-done step, but a constant thread running throughout working the rest of the steps. Even if you are doubtful right now, if you are rigorous about working all the steps, you will surely come to believe in a Power greater than yourself eventually because your life will have changed for the better.

Just for Today: Read pages 83 and 84 of the Big Book of Alcoholics Anonymous and substitute the word "debt" for "alcohol" to get an idea of the miracles you can expect if you work the Steps

February 5   It Works If You Work it

There is a TV commercial about an addiction treatment center, where the young man who is one of the owners says, "This is not a 12 step program. This works." His blanket indictment makes my heart ache for suffering compulsive debtors and spenders who might believe him and, therefore, never find the help that is freely offered throughout the world, and which has saved so many lives.

As the Big Book says on page 58: "Rarely have we seen a person fail who has thoroughly followed our path. Those who do not recover are people who cannot or will not completely give themselves to this simple program, usually men and women who are constitutionally incapable of being honest with themselves."

Just for Today: These steps work, if you are willing to think differently, to let go of control, and to be brutally honest with yourself ... that's where Step 2 comes in.

February 6   Why Am I Here?

It's easy to say that you will follow these steps when you are desperate and in horrible pain over your last spending binge or debt, you used your food money to buy a luxury item, if creditors are banging down your door and ringing your phone off the hook, or your pay has been garnished.

But it is when the pain eases up and you are craving a fix with money or when you don't like what you hear in program because it isn't what you *want* to do that the rubber meets the road in Step 2. There are definitely uncomfortable actions we must take in Recovery to right things with others and to keep our financial life clean. It can be hard going, especially in the beginning, when we have to slog through the wreckage of our past, which nobody wants to do, but is essential to reap the rewards of the program.

Step 2 is vital to *keep you* in the program. Without faith in this program, and in a Power greater than yourself, you may leave at any juncture when the going gets tough.

Just for Today: When you feel yourself resistant to difficult suggestions or when you feel about to cave into a money craving, remind yourself why you came into D.A. in the first place.

February 7 — Going to Any Length

D.A. suggests using a spending plan and tracking one's numbers as tools to prevent debting. For many people, having a spending plan and keeping their numbers is enough. But as an extreme compulsive spender as well as a debtor, my disease is cunning, baffling, and powerful in how it will trick me. So I became willing to commit my spending to someone else before I spend it and report my actual spending the next day.

If I don't do this, I end up justifying spending more than is allocated for my "wants." The dominoes fall as I take from category after category to satisfy my cravings until there's no money left for my needs and I see no choice but to debt. Following this pattern, I watched myself go from hard-won solvency with zero debt of any kind into $34,000 of credit card debt.

Without the added accountability, and honesty, open mindedness, and willingness to turn over my spending a day at a time to another recovering debtor before spending it, I slide into vagueness too easily by manipulating the spending plan and moving money from one category to another without thinking through the implications.

Just for Today: If you continue to struggle with staying solvent in D.A., consider what going to any length means for you ... and pray for the willingness to do it.

February 8 — What Kind of Recovery Do I Want?

We can choose not to debt but barely hang on by our fingernails, still acting out with money, spending in vagueness, buying based on whim and craving, living on the edge. Or, we can choose not to debt feeling more peaceful, using money in a sane and sober manner, living by a structure that makes it easier for us to recover. One way to do that is by living by our spending plan categories, not by the pile of money in our checking account, which often increases with recovery.

But before that, as a newcomer, our first opportunity to practice the principles of D.A. is to take one simple action: cut up all of our credit cards and cancel all credit accounts. Yes, this may seem terrifying, but the only way to stop debting is to stop using unsecured debt *one day at a time*. Leaving even one option open ("just for an emergency") is like keeping a bottle of liquor in your house for guests when you first get sober.

Just for Today: Do the first thing first. The rest will follow.

February 9 — Advice vs. ESH

There is a big difference between giving advice and the experience, strength, and hope (ESH) that we are encouraged to share as sponsors and in our outreach calls. Giving advice is directly telling another member or sponsee what to do. In program, our role is to guide each other to find *our own* way.

Sharing ESH is a gentle, non-threatening way to help another member hear how you or people you know have handled a similar situation. It is the way we do our 12th Step work. Most of us want to be helpful. I, for one, have a hard time saying I don't know and so reach deep down to find a solution to help. But that is not our "job" in program.

Sponsors are not therapists, seers, or coaches. And the stronger our investment is in the other person doing what we tell him or her to do, the more warning bells should go off in our head!

I have learned from painful experience to ask if someone wants feedback before launching in, and to stick to sharing my own experience around the matter rather than telling someone what to do.

Just for Today: Practice listening to others in the program as a quiet, healing presence, without feeling a need to fix the problem.

February 10   Staying the Course

What is willingness? Is it just going along when things are ok? Or is it continuing to work your program when the decision is tough and your inner voice is screaming, "I WANT IT"?

People lose their abstinence in this program when they are convinced that their Higher Power is telling them to spend money they don't have on a seemingly righteous expenditure. A good rule of thumb is that when you feel an impulse purchase or pressure for a big ticket item coming on, wait 24-48 hours before spending the money. During that time, reach out to your network and discuss the feelings with your sponsor. It is dangerous for us to try to figure this out on our own because we can easily mistake desire for good judgment.

We can start practicing by pausing when a sudden thought of spending on a small item comes to us, and asking ourselves, "Do I need this today or can it wait until tomorrow?" Waiting shows us that sometimes, what we think is our Higher Power's voice is really our own.

Just for Today: The next time you are struck with a sudden urge to spend on a specific item, take a day or two to pause before doing so, knowing that waiting will strengthen your recovery.

February 11   Going Through the Process

They say that when the pain of using is worse than the pain you're trying to avoid, you will put down the drug. For me, the pain of desire, which often made me feel as if I would die if I didn't buy the item, finally broke me down Now, I prefer going through the process of sitting through the pain, knowing that all things pass, rather than acting out when I am in the throes of it.

I know that if I give in to this raging "gotta buy it now" desperation, I will not feel the satisfaction for more than a brief moment. All that adrenaline and desperation will remain, unsatisfied because the item wasn't really the issue at all.

Just for Today: If there is a discretionary item calling you, even if you have the money available in your spending plan, be willing to wait at least 24 more hours before purchasing it to allow that desperate urge to die down.

February 12 — Sponsor Role

We are told to find a sponsor who has what we want, ask how it was achieved, and follow her direction. But we must remember that there is no perfect sponsor. Sponsors are just D.A. members working their program to the best of their ability. Sponsors are not paid to do service. They give lovingly from the heart, so we must be respectful of their time and energy, and not become overly dependent on them. This is why developing a network of D.A. members to turn to in times of crisis is a crucial part of recovery. Sponsors may need to drop us for a variety of reasons *having nothing to do with us*, including relapse or a change in health, life situation, or schedule. We can change sponsors at will, and most of us have had multiple sponsors for a variety of reasons. It's always hard to lose a sponsor or to drop one. We try not to change sponsors on a whim or due to a temporary conflict. But no one is expected to stay with a sponsor with whom we do not feel safe.

Just for Today: Remember that there must be a basic feeling of comfort and safety between sponsor and sponsee for the intimate work we do together to be effective.

February 13 — The Safety Net

We must always remember that the sponsor is just another tool in our arsenal and not our Higher Power. If we continue to work our program, reaching out to others daily, we will have a tremendous resource in case we lose our sponsor. We can turn to that network for help staying in recovery until we find another sponsor. Losing a sponsor is not an excuse to debt, but some members play on the pain suffered by the loss as a reason to do so.

None of us are saints, including sponsors! We are all just suffering debtors trying to stay in recovery and help each other one day at a time. Do not make your recovery dependent on a sponsor. People will inevitably disappoint us and are *not* the program of recovery. The steps and a relationship with our Higher Power are the program. Sponsors are just one way the message is carried.

Just for Today: If you don't have a solid D.A. network of friends, begin to reach out to others to establish this support.

February 14 — Valentine's Day: A Plea for Sanity

It's time for compulsive debtors and spenders who fall under Valentine's Day's twisted spell to see clearly through the deceptive veil that masks "the day of love." This manufactured holiday, is, in fact, a trifecta of indulgence, a promotional conspiracy between the greeting card, jewelry, and florist industries to drive consumers into guilt spree spending.

It's not the SPIRIT of Valentine's Day at issue. Any time we can express our love and gratitude to our partners is a good time. It's the way our society has connected the essence of the holiday with having to spend money to prove that you love your partner that is of concern. What a gift it would be to release your partner from feeling like he or she needs to break the bank to show how much you are loved. And for you to stop letting guilt pressure you into spending more than you can afford.

Just for Today: The D.A. program helps us learn to be more loving every day through the steps and tools. If you are working a D.A. program, remember, the best gift you can give your partner is continued recovery from compulsive debting and spending one day at a time EVERY day.

February 15   A Bridge Between

In Step 2, you turn from believing that it's "my way or the highway" to letting go of the delusion that you can control anything. This is a huge shift in thinking.

Step 1 is a thinking step. When we take that step, we finally realize what everyone around us has known for a long, long time … that our lives are a complete mess because of our addiction. Step 3 requires action by our becoming willing to do the necessary work in the rest of the steps to recover from our addiction.

But you need a bridge between awareness and action. Step 2 takes our Step 1 realization that our way has failed us miserably, and gives us the knowledge that there is a way to recovery. The way is not by self-knowledge or exerting even more control, but by coming to grips with our powerlessness and becoming teachable.

Just for Today: Remember we must keep crossing the Step 2 bridge as we work <u>all</u> of the steps to shore us up against the hard times.

February 16   10,000 Hours

According to Malcolm Gladwell in his book, *Outliers: The Story of Success*, "Practice isn't the thing you do once you're good. It's the thing you do that makes you good." He concludes that it takes 10,000 hours of practice to become an expert.

When we begin recovery, we are hopeless, and feel overwhelmed with all that we are required to do to recover from compulsive debting and spending. We fear that we will never "get it."

As with any skill worth having, recovery takes time. Luckily, in our program we have other members who have gone before us and can lead us along this path, giving us hope that with consistency and time, our situations will improve.

We must all march individually through day one, day two, and day 138 on our path in recovery. But we can be reassured by knowing that we all share a common problem ... and a common solution that will work as well for the person with little debt and lots of money as for the person with huge debt and little money.

Just for Today: Practice working the tools of the program and remind yourself that each hour you do so builds upon the previous, helping you become an expert one day at a time in your own recovery and spiritual fitness around money.

February 17   Disappointment Is Not Fatal

In recovery from compulsive debting, we can't always get our way with money. It is disappointing. But disappointment never killed anyone.

How do we act when our PRG team or sponsor doesn't give us our way? Do we throw a tantrum? Do we shut down to even considering their suggestions?

In the end, it is our money and we can choose to do what we want with it. But if we trust our PRG members and sponsor, then we also trust that our Higher Power is speaking through them to help us make tough decisions. If we made good decisions around money, we wouldn't be in this program.

Not getting our way or having to wait is definitely unpleasant. But when we follow suggestions, we learn how to have more patience. It's not a choice for us to be at peace with disappointment. Our sobriety with money is at stake. If we let disappointment turn into resentment, we will surely find a reason to leave the program and end up debting.

Just for Today: Make a commitment to being open to the suggestions of your PRG team or sponsor even if it is at odds with your momentary desire.

February 18   Pick Your Pain

I have an ever growing list of wants. It amazes me how they expand to overfill any amount of money I may have. My wants are like a greedy monster, devouring everything in sight. And the pain I feel when I don't give in can seem bottomless.

What D.A. teaches us is that all feelings pass, including the obsession to buy. But abstinence doesn't mean that life will be free of problems and pain, and that you will always get your way. Abstinence simply means you have a level playing field.

If we use money as a drug and compulsively spend, it will lead to debting. If we live above our means, in denial of what we are doing, it will lead to debting. If we live in deprivation, it will lead to resentment, which can lead to compulsive spending, which will lead to debting. In any case, living in recovery instead of acting out in disease will cause some degree of discomfort and pain.

Just for Today: Which pain do you want - the pain of disappointment and desire, which will eventually subside? Or the pain of living in our addiction, sending us spiraling down into a bottomless pit in a never-ending search to avoid discomfort that ends at the Gates of Hell?

February 19 — Making It Work

When you are committed to living by your categories, instead of by your bank balance, it can sometimes be challenging to get through a month. For instance, let's say you overspent in grocery, which really leaves you tight toward the end of the month. In that case, you have two recovery choices. You can either work with your sponsor to move money from another category to cover the amount you will need to get you to the end of the month. Or you can accept the situation as it is and make it work one day at time until the next month.

While both paths keep you in recovery, it can be a humbling and spiritually inspiring experience to commit to the latter course. In that case, you might scrounge through your cupboard and freezer to use up food that is not your first choice to eat. Eating those cans of tuna and frozen vegetables shows a willingness to live by the main principle of this program, which is to live within our means. Each category is a microcosm of that overall approach. Plus, you are learning to use what you have, rather than just accumulating more and more.

Just for Today: If you run short in a category, consider waiting it out until the next month ... without thinking that it is deprivation.

February 20   A Grateful Heart

It is easy to be grateful when things are going our way. But it is when life is throwing us curve balls that finding gratitude is most important.

They say that a grateful heart doesn't binge. But it's so hard to see any light when there is a blanket of sorrow or self-pity covering us. Still, when we even peek out from under that covering, the light of gratitude can flood in and change our perspective.

No one says we must *feel* the gratitude. Just recognizing the blessings in our lives opens the door for more of the good stuff. No matter how bleak the future seems, there is always *something* in the present for which we can be grateful.

Just for Today: Start a habit of writing down five gratitudes daily, no matter how you feel.

February 21   Cost vs. Price

If we spend according to our obsession despite what we know about recovery, there is no question that another item will take the place of the one we just bought sooner, rather than later. And once we convince ourselves that it is ok to do this, what will stop us from moving money around in our categories as we see fit? And then, how easy it will be to convince ourselves that we are doing fine and don't need a sponsor ... or this program, for that matter. And then, how long will it be until we find an excuse to use a credit card for an item that costs more than our available cash that we MUST have or we WILL DIE? And then, the horror and humiliation we'll experience when the realization of what we have destroyed will be putty in the hands of our disease, which just wants to have fun, its sick, dank, dark, depraved idea of fun. And then, we won't be able to stop the process.

If we spend out of self-will and obsession, our disease, seeing it can have its way with us by bullying us with desire, won't let up. Once we give in, we will surely feel remorse, but it will be drowned out by the screams of our craving body for more, more, more, until we are done in for good.

Just for Today: Is the cost of buying in obsession worth the price?

February 22   A Psychic Change

What is this psychic change? It is the sure knowing, that came first with faith and later with belief from our own experience, that if we don't give in to compulsive spending and debting, then our Higher Power will remove the obsession.

The obsession will come back and try again, but if we turn to our program and Higher Power each and every time, it will pass. Never once can we fool ourselves that we can use a credit card or spend like others with impunity.

Thankfully, we have a network of people surrounding us in recovery to help us get through it. But if, instead, we fall prey to that delusion, we will repeat that endless cycle and lose all that we have gained materially, spiritually, and emotionally in recovery.

Just for Today: We must remember that the addiction to debting and spending is serious. In fact, it's deadly. So when we think of bucking our sponsor or PRG team members when we are in obsession, we remind ourselves that our Higher Power works through others to keep us in recovery ... and pause to reconsider our plans.

February 23 — Delayed Gratification

I have to admit that I have not yet been freed from the obsession for buying. However, I'm grateful to have learned how to get through it abstinently and distance myself from that unbearable feeling more quickly.

Yes, one can be abstinent and in obsession. The key is *not* to make a purchase when you are having that experience. Instead, use those feelings as an opportunity to practice delayed gratification and patience. Another way to help yourself as you go through this process is by focusing on gratitude for what you do have.

The problem is that I feel that I will die, actually die, if I don't get what I want the moment I want it. But if I don't give in to it, eventually, hours, days, weeks, maybe months later, it passes. And by not giving into it, I get to see the desire morph and sometimes disappear completely! I've often regretted a purchase, but never regretted waiting.

Just for Today: Asking yourself, "Can this wait until tomorrow?" is one of the most healing practices in D.A..

February 24 — Change of Speech

By simply becoming aware of what we say and how we say it, we take a huge step toward doing our part in removing many of our character defects, such as interrupting, anger, resentment, gossip, and criticism. To do this, we must first become conscious of what leads up to what we say. Negative speech is always preceded by an emotion, and it is in that split second before expressing ourselves verbally (or pressing the Send button) that we can grow spiritually and these defects can begin to be healed internally. There is an expression that gets to the heart of this practice: "Between the spark and the flame, pause and ask if it will be beneficial to express." With compulsive debting and spending, this is the moment when we are buffeted by obsession, but just before we act out. It feels so difficult to recognize, but it *can* be learned. By pausing in that moment, we have the opportunity to stop the cycle of addiction. Equally, lashing out in anger, interrupting, and more are all habitual patterns that can also be replaced by healthier reactions *if* we are willing to sit in the discomfort that precedes the outburst instead of dumping it onto another person.

Just for Today: Can I sit with and accept my feelings without having to vent them?

February 25 — Lending Money

What about the other side of debting ... lending money? Recently, I wrote Debtors Anonymous to find out what they think, and they responded by saying they have no official opinion on lending money.

It's a slippery slope. As a compulsive spender, I could easily find ways to justify spending that I cannot afford. I remember hearing that you should only lend money with the thought that it is a gift because it's as likely as not that you won't be paid back. So *never* lend more than you can afford to lose. If you watch TV court shows, you know how often loans aren't repaid!

What about signing as a guarantor on someone's cell phone account, car loan, rental agreement, etc.? The bottom line is that you, as the guarantor, are responsible if the person doesn't pay, and that means you have taken on a new debt if they fail to keep their commitment. Is it worth risking your solvency to keep the peace?

Just for Today: When we act with integrity in Recovery, our boundaries may be at odds with others' desires, but we can find peace knowing that we have made a decision based on sober thinking.

February 26   Accepting the Unacceptable

We rarely say "why me" when the fabulous and miraculous occur. So, perhaps we can shift our thinking when the opposite presents in our lives. This takes a lot of practice, willingness, and awareness to accomplish. Acceptance is not easy during times of turmoil and trial. Maybe start with the small things that tweak you … the temporary setbacks. If someone cuts you off while driving, keep it in perspective.

It is important to practice our program of acceptance on small issues that pass. That is the first step in learning to better handle and find peace when something truly life-changing happens.

Settling in for the long haul with a tragic truth is far more difficult when the prevailing sentiment is rage and self-pity once the grieving has worn itself out and life continues. Grieving is an indispensable step we take when tragedy strikes. But the question is how to live in recovery when facing adversity that is here to stay.

Just for Today: Turn to, and deeply ponder, the Serenity Prayer, a tried and true tool to help manage difficult situations.

February 27   What You Cannot Change

They say, "a grateful heart doesn't pick up." When you get upset over things outside of your control, try turning your attention to gratitude for what you do have. In D.A., gratitude is an important component in the prevention of resentment and anger build-up. As the Big Book says on page 66, "If we were to live, we had to be free of anger. The grouch and the brainstorm were not for us. They may be the dubious luxury of normal men, but for alcoholics these things are poison."

Unfortunately, it's not a choice for compulsive debtors either. So we must find the way to peace and acceptance no matter how bad the situation is. We may not be able to change the circumstance, but we can surely change ourselves and our attitude about it. All it takes is willingness to do so. Service can be a help as well. When we reach out to others, we often see that their plight is worse, plus, it takes us out of our poisonous self-centered self-pity.

Just for Today: Next time you get worked up over a problem, pick up the phone and make a call. Talk about your problems and listen to someone else's. Together, you may find a relief that you couldn't have imagined had you isolated yourself.

February 28 — Hope

We come into program broken, having hit a bottom. It may take a while to turn this around. We have taken the first step, where we admit we are powerless over debting. In Step 2, we come to believe that we can be restored to sanity by a Power greater than ourselves. Knowing that we *can* be saved from our addiction even if we don't yet experience it is what hope is all about.

Still, when we first reach Step 2, we are in that tough place where we see the truth of our problem and know there is a solution, but we don't yet know what to do about it.

When we find ourselves drowning in self-pity, thinking there is no way out of our situation, the hope of Step 2 can make us hang on. We can already take action during these moments by making an outreach call, speaking with our sponsor, or having a PRG. Those who have gone before us may give us ideas that we hadn't considered ... if we are open to them. They may not be the ideas that we want to hear, but if we are willing to follow direction, we might just be led out of the darkness.

Just for Today: Hope is seeing that there is a light at the end of the tunnel.

February 29 — The Fine Print

In this marketing driven world, we may receive offers that look too good to be true. Unfortunately, that old adage often proves to be the case. Where before, we leapt off the cliff without taking a peek at what was waiting for us below, in recovery, we learn to read the fine print so we don't sink into consumer quicksand. In particular, we look for exclusions, limitations, commitments, pre-existing conditions, and additional charges and fees. Examples where these issues apply include exercise equipment, cars, cable TV, career certification, insurance, and medical cures. We may feel a tug to take advantage of the offer without taking the time to investigate further. After all, we don't want to wait and the fine print is difficult to read. But in recovery from compulsive debting and spending, we no longer act in a knee-jerk manner especially when feeling pressured to buy. We have learned to pause before making major investments so that we can determine whether we are making a sober decision. Now, we are becoming informed consumers who no longer wake up with buyer's remorse.

Just for Today: Are you willing to take the time to read the fine print to ensure that what you're actually getting is what you really want?

March 1 — Diving into Recovery

In Step 3, we "made a decision to turn our will and our lives over to the care of God *as we understood Him*."

On paper, taking Step 3 seems quite esoteric. How, exactly, do we turn our will and lives over? It's simple. If we believe that the path to recovery is in the Steps, turning our will and lives over to this Higher Power just means that we follow the instructions for Steps 4-12. So the decision we make in Step 3 is essentially a contract to work the remaining steps.

Another way to look at this is that Step 3 is the diving board off of which we jump into the cold water of Step 4. Yet, walking out to the end of the board and taking that leap is essential if we are to find the recovery offered by D.A..

Just for Today: Don't overcomplicate the program. Just move forward and follow directions.

March 2 — Now

"Now" is a crucial word in recovery. It is dangerous when it means awakening the beast of craving and fear in an obsession to spend. It is the most beautiful and perfect word to describe how to live our lives and what to focus on. It is amazing how one word can be both destructive and life-giving at the same time.

In disease, we lived unconsciously around time and money. We borrowed money pretending it was ours, and never understood that we couldn't borrow time, believing that we could.

When we live in now, without expectation, there is plenty of time. When we savor each moment, instead of waiting for the next in anticipation of something better, we have enough. In the same way, when we live in gratitude instead of obsessing over what we want to buy next, we are enough.

Just for Today: Help me enjoy the positive aspects of "Now" and release the insistent, grasping, demanding side.

March 3 — Peaceful Means

When I was a "big spender," throwing money around for gifts, dinners, etc., I was never jealous of others because I lived in the delusion that I had lots of money. When the blunt truth of my financial limits became clear in recovery, I felt much pain when I couldn't pick up the tab or buy a gift. That's when I began to wriggle uncomfortably in what I thought were the shackles of recovery. I started to compare myself to others who didn't have to think twice about buying a car, much less dinner, and self-pity grew. Eventually, I understood the truth. Because I no longer incur unsecured debt, I am free in a way that too many are not, those who are still slaves to their credit cards and "stuff," who live beyond their means, with crushing financial pressure. Today, I am relieved that I don't have to live that way. Today I live by my spending plan, within my financial limits. I cherish those limits and living by them because the gifts I receive far outweigh any material belongings I might accrue otherwise. Today, I no longer feed the craving monster any time it demands food. There is far more peace that way. And I know that I am enough when I live in peace.

Just for Today: Can you feel the relief of your financial limits?

March 4   Vision or Self-Will

In D.A., there is lots of talk about visions, which is a wonderful by-product of recovery. However, sometimes people are convinced that they must achieve their visions today, despite the fact that they cannot fund them. In recovery from compulsive debting, living by our spending plan is a core component of our spiritual path. Until there is money available, we don't buy it. It's that simple. "Visions" can be obsession in disguise when it means being unwilling to wait and instead spending down our savings, borrowing from our 401K, or refinancing our mortgage to achieve a discretionary goal. In this case, it's just another way our disease is trying to convince us to veer from our recovery path. When we can find peace with waiting, though we may have a preference to get going now, that is in keeping with a recovery life. In D.A., visions are not about *creating* our own destiny (that is self-will, which is what brought many of us to our knees in the first place), but allowing our life to unfold as our Higher Power sees fit, being *open* to finding our passion, and *willing* to achieve it in a recovery way.

Just for Today: Do you believe that if it is your Higher Power's will, you will be able to fund your visions without debting or depleting your savings?

March 5 — Dominoes

I do not move money between overall categories in my spending plan on my own. This is where the rubber meets the road in recovery for me. For instance, it works for me to choose to use Food money for either restaurant or grocery. But if I decide on my own to take from food to pay for gas, then I may need to take from clothing to pay for food.

Maybe I decide to take money from life insurance to pay for clothing instead of waiting until next month when I have enough money for the purchase. And then, when I need to pay my insurance bill, I'm short because I moved the money.

While this is not debting, it's definitely not recovery behavior for me, and is a slippery slope toward relapse. However, there is a difference between moving money for discretionary items rather than waiting, and ensuring our needs are met. So, if I am short in gas or food, both of which I need, and talk to my sponsor about it, we can make a measured decision in choosing which category is appropriate to cover the expense with the least amount of fallout.

Just for Today: If you do not have enough money in a category, consider having a PRG to better fund it.

March 6 — PRG Humility

Pressure Relief Groups (PRGs) are great for keeping me humble and solving problems that seem insurmountable. Sometimes I go into them with an agenda. That rarely works out well, as my mind is not right about money and it is the wisdom of hearing two others in program come together that can convince me of the error of my ways if that is the case (as it often is).

At other times, I come into a PRG with a problem that I am certain has no solution and my team figures one out. It is truly a miraculous process where my Higher Power speaks through others.

Sometimes, you may not have a PRG team that works for you. But don't stop trying to find a team that is a good fit because, when you do find that team, it's an invaluable part of this process. We are not meant to do this on our own, and dealing with the physical aspects of money can be especially raw for us.

Just for Today: If you don't have a PRG team, begin reaching out for one. If you do, schedule a PRG when you need help.

March 7 — Feelings Aren't Facts

I feel that I will die, actually die, if I don't get what I want the moment I want it. It used to be a horrifying feeling. Now, it's unpleasant, but I have learned to recognize it for what it is a lot sooner ... my disease trying to coerce me into relapse.

That feeling of obsession blankets me. It convinces me that whatever the object of the obsession, I *must* have it in order to live.

But...

If I don't give in to it, eventually, hours, days, weeks, maybe months later, the obsession passes. By not giving into it, I also get to see the desire morph. Sometimes I watch, amused, as one object of obsession is replaced by another and another and another during the wait, so that by the time the feeling has subsided, I no longer even want the original object anymore! If you experience such emotions around spending or when you get a windfall, you can help yourself through this process of balancing obsession with recovery by focusing on gratitude. When we live in gratitude, and in the present moment, it is much easier to release obsession. They say a grateful heart doesn't binge. I think that's because we open ourselves to feel the true, pure joy of recovery that no money can buy.

Just for Today: Surrender to waiting when in the throes of obsession.

March 8 — Keeping Numbers As a Spiritual Path

Some D.A. members feel terrified at the prospect of working with numbers, and dread the "tedious" process of keeping a spending plan up-to-date. But it is in the act of keeping our numbers and living within our spending plan that recovery unfolds. As with any spiritual discipline, it takes time to learn and a commitment to consistent practice to see positive results. For instance, T'ai Chi involves watching the slightest movement, and mindfulness meditation focuses on every thought, emotion, and feeling. Those who learn and practice these disciplines on a regular basis find tremendous spiritual benefits. It's no different with our spiritual discipline. Many of us come into D.A. broken, and totally vague about our money. It will take time and effort to learn this new way of life. But those who only sporadically reconcile with their bank account and rarely update their spending plan find themselves fixing problems that arise from such vagueness, creating unnecessary frustration. Those who commit to the spiritual discipline of the spending plan on a regular basis feel the calm and peace resulting from this practice.

Just for Today: If you resent keeping your numbers, can you choose to look at the process as a spiritual practice instead?

March 9   Why Me?

When we start feeling sorry for ourselves, whether about finances, health, or relationships, it is easy to spiral downward, which can lead to debting or other self-destructive behaviors. Someone facing a terminal illness once said that she sank into depression thinking "why me?" But then, the thought came to her, "why not me?"

Is there anyone on this planet, no matter how great their life looks to us, who doesn't experience some type of aggravation, dilemma, and tragedy in their life? The great equalizer is that every one of us will be leaving this planet at some undetermined time … and whatever we have accumulated on this earth isn't going with us.

Knowing that everyone faces challenges, we can choose to fall apart at the least inconvenience, bemoaning our lot in life … or we can truly understand that life involves some degree of challenge for everyone. So, rather than looking at ourselves as victims, maybe we can find comfort in knowing that we are not alone, no matter what adversity we face, and remember that there are people who have withstood far worse.

Just for Today: If you begin to sink into self-pity and "why me," stop and think, "why not me," and then, make a call to someone you can help.

March 10 — Equanimity

Equanimity is defined as "mental or emotional stability or composure, especially under tension or strain" (Dictionary.com). These are the qualities we strive for in recovery from compulsive debting. Nothing in that definition specifically addresses money, yet without equanimity, we are "dry drunks" with our wallet hanging out of our pocket.

Without equanimity, we can obsess about buying, and compulsively spend even within our means, which *can* lead us into a binge. And don't we want peace of mind around money? That is why working all the steps is so vital. The purpose of the steps is to help us develop equanimity, not just around money, but in our relations with others and in how we walk in the world. Through equanimity, we express the person our Higher Power wants us to be. When we have mental calm in difficult situations, we can better connect with that Higher Power to make difficult decisions. When we maintain evenness of temper in a challenging interaction, we are channeling the unconditional love of our Higher Power.

Just for today: Recognize that equanimity is an achievable goal. Even if we don't reach it in all situations, striving for it can help us stay in recovery.

March 11 — Measures of Progress

Recovering D.A. members experience signposts that are measures of their progress. For instance, they no longer try to find excuses to spend down their savings. They have willingness to wait before purchasing if their sponsor or PRG team advises them to do so … with less petulance. More often, they feel sane around money and spending. They do not react in a knee-jerk fashion when they see the word "sale." They recoil when they recognize that they are trying to justify spending when they don't have available funds, and are aware a lot sooner. More and more, they see a spending obsession coming on and shut it down instead of romancing the desire. But they are willing to ask for help when in the grips of a purchasing obsession so that they can be restored to their right mind before acting on the impulse.

Just for Today: What measures of progress do you see in your recovery?

March 12 — Sales Mentality

Living by a spending plan frees us from the hold sales have on us because in recovery, we plan our spending and base it on available money instead of buying *because* there's a sale.

Yes, we may feel a painful twinge from our old way of thinking, but in recovery, we know the danger of the sale mentality. In the same way, it's not always sober to stock up at the grocery store when something is on sale. For many of us, when we do that, we are left short for the current month's groceries.

In recovery, we no longer view shopping as recreation or a grazing activity. And we let go of that "gotta have it now or it's gone" mentality if we want to be free of suffering around this issue. In recovery, we know there is always another sale, and we know that by waiting until we have the cash, our purchase will be more sober and enjoyable even if the item is *not* on sale.

Just for Today: If you feel triggered to buy a sale item you hadn't thought about purchasing previously, talk to your sponsor or network, and do some writing around it.

March 13   Justice and Compassion

Page 66 of the Big Book states, "It is plain that a life which includes deep resentment leads only to futility and unhappiness." If we are to have any peace, we must find a way to meet injustice with compassion. Here's why. When we see something we consider unjust, we feel ourselves getting all riled up. Adrenaline begins to flow and self-righteous indignation is the result, which can lead to debting as a release.

So we need to learn a new way of reacting if we are to stay sober with money. That is a tall task for addicts who have perfected the art of blaming others for their problems. Even in recovery, we may take responsibility for what happens in our own life, but we have often used the excuse of bigger injustice as a way to get high on adrenaline and self-righteous indignation. We know that our body feels beat up after a bout of spewing out poison, even if it feels justified. The Big Book tells us we don't have to do so.

Just for Today: When we feel our blood boiling over injustice, stay quiet. By not releasing the poisonous thought into the universe, we begin to learn how to meet justice with compassion.

March 14   Recovering or Recovered?

"We, of Alcoholics Anonymous, are more than one hundred men and women who have recovered from a seemingly hopeless state of mind and body." (Big Book's Foreword to the First Edition). Someone suggested that when the obsession has been lifted, when we recoil as from a hot flame, when we are no longer tempted to act out on our addiction, then it is appropriate to say we are recovered. Recovered does *not* mean cured, nor does it mean that we are normal or can walk away from program. Quite the reverse is true. They say the further you are from your last binge, the closer you are to your next. So we must stay even closer to program.

Many of us still obsess occasionally, so we may be more comfortable saying that we are *in recovery* from compulsive debting because we stay sober with money and debt despite those occasional problems. We are learning a new way of living, and doing our part in partnership with our Higher Power. In the end, it's all just semantics. *Recovering* or *recovered*, as long as we do today what we did yesterday with money, we will never incur new unsecured debt. And *that* is Recovery.

Just for Today: I pray that God will keep me walking the path of recovery until and after I am recovered from my hopeless condition regarding money and debt.

March 15   Giving Away Our Power

It is the D.A. group as a whole through which our Higher Power speaks. If we give our sponsor all that power over us, we will end up feeling resentful, because people are imperfect and may disappoint us at some point. We need to understand that each of us is here to save our own life, first and foremost. When we criticize our sponsors, we need to consider how far they have come from where they started. We are told that we can change sponsors at will. This sounds light and uncomplicated, but in reality, it is rarely so easy. We develop deep relationships with our sponsors and sponsees, often blurring the line between friendship and the sponsor/sponsee relationship. We get a sponsor so we can be abstinent and free from debt one day at a time. Our sponsors guide us on this journey. They say that we should get a sponsor who has what we want and ask how it was achieved. The next sentence is only implied – then we follow direction. If the sponsor no longer has what we want, then we are free to move on. Otherwise, we do what is asked of us, even when challenging. But, if necessary, we *can* extricate ourselves from either side of this relationship with kindness and integrity.

Just for Today: Remember that your sponsor is just another compulsive debtor in recovery one day at a time.

March 16   Giving PRGs Gently

Members of a PRG team have an obligation to practice active listening when serving on a PRG. We make sure we hear and validate the recipient's concerns before launching in with our ideas. It is always helpful when both team members are in agreement about a course of action, especially when it is in conflict with the recipient's desire. We must be conscious of the fact that there is a big difference in gently guiding a member to doing what may be hard, and having an agenda that says our way is the only way.

Even though we don't get paid to give this service, as a PRG team member we must be cognizant of how strongly we can impact others. We are all here to recover *and* share our ESH as part of this path of service. But we want to be ever mindful of *how* we do so, or we might inadvertently turn a member off to the incredible process a PRG can be or send them back out there to use because they don't feel safe. Though we cannot control others' feelings, we can still do our best to act as kindly as possible, knowing that PRGs are often a situation in which people feel extremely vulnerable and frightened.

Just for Today: If we ever receive a PRG where we feel beaten down and not heard, we can be assured that this is the exception, not the rule.

March 17 — Sharing ESH Consciously

In D.A., members are not counselors, seers, financial advisors, or life coaches (though we may work in that field outside of D.A.). We are just compulsive debtors in recovery one day at a time sharing our experience, strength, and hope with others to help them recover. Some of us may feel it is our responsibility to solve others' problems. In doing so, we may cause more pain if the person isn't ready … or we are wrong.

While sponsors are responsible for guiding sponsees regarding money and working the steps, sponsees may need to discuss other types of issues as well. In addition, outreach calls are also a venue for sharing. In either case, it is always wise to ask if the person wants our experience, strength, and hope (ESH) or just needs to vent. If he says yes, we can share our ESH, but we are always careful not to fall into advice-giving. If we have no ESH in that circumstance, then we can be honest about it. As well, if the person doesn't want feedback, we can just listen offering our hope that a solution is revealed. Most importantly, we do not allow ourselves to get riled up thinking about how we could fix the member if he would *only* listen.

Just for Today: Do you understand that service to others is about support, not problem-solving? Problem solving is the job of their Higher Power.

March 18 — Recovery Blueprint

Our spending plan is the blueprint for the physical part of this program, and the Big Book and D.A. literature contain instructions for the spiritual side. If we are honest and diligent about sticking to our spending plan, and rigorous in keeping it up to date, we will never debt again. When we look at our spending plan, we can see clearly on paper how much money we have, to the penny, and how much, to the penny, is available in any category. If an emergency comes up, the spending plan becomes the means by which our PRG team can help us find the money to cover it. We may have money available in a Contingency category. But if that isn't enough, rather than immediately turning to our savings, we can make choices to take money that has accumulated in discretionary categories to cover the emergency. While we do not fund our discretionary categories intending to use the accumulated money for other purposes, we also live life life's terms and recognize that our plans may not always work out as we wish. Yes, there is disappointment in having to take from these categories, but the miracle of paying our way without debting or spending down savings is crystal clear, and we know that the categories will accrue again.

Just for Today: Are you rigorous in keeping your spending plan up-to-date?

March 19 — PRG Parameters

A PRG is not the place to request financial advice, such as how to get the best interest rates or where to invest your money. PRG team members are not professional financial planners, just other addicts in recovery one day at a time. They are *not* your Higher Power.

Though your PRG team is not your Higher Power, your Higher Power may speak through them. You will have to learn, through trial and error, when resistance is your disease acting up and when it is truly the result of problematic feedback.

It was a stroke of genius to ensure PRGs are made up of two other members. Generally, if two people agree, the feedback is more likely to be accurate, especially if we are kicking and screaming in defiance. In this case, it's more likely than not to just be our disease acting up.

Just for Today: If you feel defiant about following a suggestion from your PRG team, seek clarity by meditating so you can hear your Higher Power's voice over the cries of your desire.

March 20 — Jumping Off a Cliff

There is a fine line between not giving advice and standing by while someone jumps off a cliff. While we don't want to give advice, it is, nevertheless, vital for us to live in our own truth about recovery when we see catastrophe about to occur. For instance, if someone called to talk about getting a second mortgage on her house so she could train for a new career, my truth would be to lovingly tell the member that I don't use debt, even secured debt, as a way to fund discretionary items, even career training. This would open a Pandora's Box and lead me down the slippery slope into full-blown spending and debting. However, we are not anyone's Higher Power. If this member was a D.A. long-timer who had been working with a PRG team on this idea for years, had paid off her debts, and worked her program diligently, it might be the right path for her. But, if she just thought up this idea, it would trigger warning bells. Even so, there is no justification for advice-giving in D.A.. Instead, we do our best to share our ESH and offer suggestions if asked, but we do not judge or tell someone what to do.

Just for Today: The next time you find yourself winding up to give advice, take a moment to breathe and feel if this is coming from a place of ESH or imposing your will.

March 21   Communicating with Creditors

D.A. tells us that we take care of our basic needs before we pay our creditors, which means that some members cannot afford to make even a minimal payment toward their debts at first. However, D.A. also suggests that we communicate with our creditors instead of living in vagueness and fear. That is not the same as being intimidated into paying more than we can afford. If we have a solid spending plan developed with the help of a PRG team, we will be confident in the amount we can pay, if we can pay at all. *We never promise to pay more than we can afford.* A common temptation is to pay—or promise to pay—more than we can afford. Both may damage our relationships with our creditors. Worse, paying too much might lead us to incur new, unsecured debt. To avoid that, we do not pay so much that we neglect our own needs. The problem with paying our debt first is that if we live in deprivation for too long, we will surely rebel, and debting will be soon to follow. That is why budgets don't work for us and why it is vital to develop a spending plan with our PRG team as soon as possible. We may *think* we won't rebel living on a tightrope. But that is not the case, as borne out by many D.A. members' experiences.

Just for Today: We do not deplete our savings as the way to eliminate the pain of owing our debts.

March 22 — Resentments & Forgiveness

We can't ignore resentments away. They just burrow deeper. Resentment feels dark, corrosive, and painful, destroying everything in its path. Forgiveness feels light, joyous, and freeing.

Resentment kills other relationships as collateral damage. Forgiveness heals.

Resentment causes us to take actions that are counter to our recovery. Forgiveness brings us closer to our Higher Power and a spiritual peace.

Resentment causes addicts to pick up to try and shut out the pain. Forgiveness grows a grateful heart that stays sober.

There is a road to recovery and a road to relapse. Each time we come to a fork in that road, we can make a choice.

Just for Today: If you find yourself overwhelmed with resentment, stop a moment and think about which path you're going to follow. And remember that taking "Relapse Road" has few U-turns.

March 23 — Fear Rules

Fear rules my life too often. My last 4th Step Fear sheet grew so large that eventually, I just wrote "Everything." Change, stagnation, death, life, pain, something happening to people I love, not having enough, getting what I want, not getting what I want. The list is endless.

Many of us are tormented by fears, big and small, now that we don't have the luxury of diving into our addiction to blot it out. Maybe it's just our automatic reaction to anything other than stasis once we are sober with money.

No matter how good things may be at any given moment, for many of us, if our mind goes to the idea of something going wrong in the future, we get frightened and can work ourselves into a frenzy about it.

What changed? Our mind changed.

Program teaches us that we can change our mind back. Just as we learn not to obsess about spending, we can choose not to romance the thought of potential future doom. Instead, we can pull ourselves back into this day, this moment, when all is fundamentally well.

Just for Today: Why ruin a perfectly good day by romancing fear of the future?

March 24 — Pink Clouds

Some people experience what's called a "pink cloud" in early recovery. It's a euphoric feeling of optimism and confidence that we've kicked the addiction with ease. Conversely, some people never experience a pink cloud and think it means there's something wrong with how they're working the program.

But a "pink cloud" is just a passing high, an illusion. Eventually, those of us on a "pink cloud" will be faced with one or more challenges that will jolt us out of that luscious state of mind. If we aren't prepared, the pain and disappointment when the "pink cloud" is gone can lead us back into compulsive debting and spending.

Real recovery, and the joy it brings, takes hard work and builds one day at a time. There are no shortcuts.

Just for Today: With or without a "pink cloud," recovery is about staying solvent no matter what.

March 25   Our Legacy

Many people use distraction to keep from facing the one unpredictable inevitability of life ... the end of it. Our material-driven society is fraught with acquiring goods ... a more, more, more philosophy, as if focusing on the bright and shiny object changes the reality of the world. For some of us, debting and spending was a way to achieve immortality. Many of us yearned to leave something behind so we wouldn't be forgotten. We were the big spender always picking up the tab. Or we invested our money in becoming famous or glamorous or sought after. For some, material acquisitions (a bigger big screen TV, a cooler car) were a way to keep the thoughts at bay. And for others, the race to get "the most" made them feel powerful. But the truth is, the moment we take our last breath, it won't matter anymore. In recovery, our focus in life shifts from what we can get to what we can give. We become more service-oriented and less self-centered. We make a difference in the lives of others, leaving behind a legacy of good deeds that dwarfs any self-seeking schemes for immortality we had in the past.

Just for Today: Are we right-minded about the legacy we want to leave?

March 26 — A Slight Nudge

I have no clue where I got the idea that my intuition would be a blaring trumpet or a robot-like voice shouting "Danger! Danger!" Or that my Higher Power would literally speak to me in conversational tones, saying, for instance, "Look here, my child, definitely DON'T do that." I mistakenly thought that the whispers of intuition were louder than the cries of distraction. The truth is that the more ruckus we generate inside and outside of ourselves, the less likely it is that we will hear that "still, small voice."

For some of us, intuition manifests as a nudging, a slight discomfort in our gut, a warm gnawing that slightly offsets our intent to do something. However your own intuition manifests, listening for, and to, your intuition may have to be a choice if it is subtle in nature and can't compete with desire's loud cries. Working Step 11, which suggests prayer and meditation, are ways we learn to quiet ourselves so we can hear our intuition.

Just for Today: Are you aware of how your intuition speaks to you?

March 27 — A Matter of Perspective

D.A. recommends three categories to keep us balanced between present and future needs.
* A Prudent Reserve is funded with six months of living expenses in the event that we lose our job or become disabled.
* A Contingency category contains money for emergencies, such as an unexpected house repair.
* The Savings category is for our future and retirement.

Few of us will be able to fully fund these categories or even fund them monthly at first. The key is that we work at it. Even saving $1/month is a step in the right direction. One of the miracles of D.A. is that surprisingly good things often happen once we make the effort to do what is suggested, such as receiving an unexpected windfall or a bonus at work. Now that we fund these savings categories, we must develop a proper view about them, and shift our perspective if we are secretly thinking that we will use this money for other purposes once it has accumulated. Though a crisis may arise that blows our plans to pieces, we do not view this accumulation of cash as a way to fund some discretionary item or service. Instead, we create categories to save for those items as well.

Just for Today: Am I funding my future as well as my present?

March 28   Triggers

As we progress in recovery, we become more conscious of what sets us up to debt or compulsively spend, and learn ways to either avoid the trigger or deal with it soberly. If sales tweak us, we can remove ourselves from email lists, throw out newspaper flyers without reading them, stop watching shopping channels on TV, make a daily commitment not to surf the web for items we aren't planning to purchase, and stop hanging out at the mall for entertainment. We can bookend with another D.A. member if we know we will be in a trigger situation we cannot avoid, such as having to make a purchase in certain stores or if we know we will feel compelled to pick up the restaurant tab for everyone when we can't afford it. When unexpectedly in a situation that is triggering us, we can excuse ourselves for a moment and make a phone call or simply connect with our Higher Power mentally and pray for willingness to stay abstinent through the situation. These new behaviors may be challenging to adhere to at first as we break old habits, but it is far better to face the discomfort than continue to flirt with danger.

Just for Today: It is unreasonable to expect that we will never react to our triggers. But with the help of our program tools and network, we can make it easier on ourselves to stay abstinent despite them.

March 29   Why Is This Happening to Me?

When things don't go our way, we can choose how we view the situation. We don't have to launch into self-pity. Someone once suggested, "Nothing is happening *to* me. Nothing has ever happened *to* me. Nothing *will* ever happen *to* me. Life is happening and I am simply a part of it."

There is tremendous relief in shifting our perspective when things go wrong. Each of us has our own trials and tribulations, but shake the world up and your tribulations could just as easily be someone else's. When we hear of a stranger's problems, we do not feel the same level of emotion as we would if we were experiencing the same situation. The fact is, if we can step out of our own pain, even briefly, we can see that our attitude can shift around it. Daily meditation, as suggested in Step 11, is a great practice for doing this type of work. When we stop viewing ourselves as victims, there is strength and calm in how we handle adversity.

Just for Today: When small annoyances, or even tragedy, occurs in your life, trying to shift your perspective just a bit can relieve at least a small part of your suffering.

March 30   The Glittering Prize

"When the 12th step is seen in its full implication, it is really talking about the kind of love that has no price tag at all." Page 106, the 12&12. It's so hard to let go of expectations; to give without thought of receiving; to love those we can't stand … or at least be civil to them. On our recovery path, we seek to become more in tune with the spirit. We want to feel better, not just become better. We want to be free of anger, to be calm in the face of the storm. We want to *feel* more spiritual, not just do the right thing and still experience negative emotions. But that is part and parcel of giving without expectation. There is a story that speaks to this point about Mother Theresa responding to a monk's anguish because he didn't feel the presence of God. She basically said, "so what," adding that she didn't feel God's presence most of the time either. It's terrific when we get the spiritual goodies we strive for, peace, calm, and joy. It's fabulous when our efforts are rewarded by getting the job we want, the house we want, the partner we want.

Just for Today: Let us remember that in recovery, we know we must continue doing the right thing whether we get the glittering prizes or not in order to stay sober with money.

March 31 — Faith

Faith is not the same as belief. In fact, faith, which is experiential, comes before belief, which is theoretical. Newcomers to D.A. act on faith. They take direction because they see others have experienced relief from this disease by working the steps. Belief comes when we experience the miracles of the program for ourselves.

When newcomers get demoralized or scared, doubting the efficacy of the program, they can get to a meeting or call someone who has been in program awhile and ask them about the miracles they have experienced. Taking these actions is how we stay the course before we experience belief.

Just for Today: I can work the program to the best of my ability, knowing that the miracles others have experienced can happen to me if I don't give up

April 1 — Lights, Camera, Action

First we illuminate, then we examine, and finally, we are lead directly into action, as described on page 63 of the Big Book (substituting the word "money" or "debt" as appropriate): "Next we launched out on a course of vigorous action, the first step of which is a personal housecleaning, which many of us had never attempted.

Though our decision was a vital and crucial step, it could have little permanent effect unless at once followed by a strenuous effort to face, and to be rid of, the things in ourselves which had been blocking us. Our liquor was but a symptom. So we had to get down to causes and conditions."

Many become terrified and paralyzed when faced with the seeming enormity of the task of Step 4. But it is far less daunting when you get some simple direction on how to approach it.

Just for Today: This "vigorous course of action" continues through working the rest of the steps. We come back to the first three steps at times of doubt to remind us of why we are in this program in the first place.

April 2 — Stall Tactics

For me, doubt and argument are simply ways the disease of compulsive debting and spending keeps me from recovery. When I argue, it's just a stalling tactic that keeps me from having to do something I don't want to do, just like my compulsive debting and spending were.

The bottom line is … it's ok to doubt … as long as you don't let it keep you from moving into Step 4 and the rest of the steps. A lot of people stall and stall, taking months, if not years to complete this step. Some people even leave the program due to their terror of picking up the pen to begin!

But completing the 4th Step doesn't have to be the crushing emotional experience we fear, and it can be completed in just days or weeks by simply following the directions on pages 64-71 of the Big Book!

Just for Today: Read pages 64-71 of the Big Book. Remember that writing down information about our past and present doesn't have to entail reliving it.

April 3 — Attitude

Step 4 can be an exuberant, freeing exercise instead of the awful heart-grinding experience many fear, if approached as a "fact-finding" expedition, and not an unwilling unearthing of hidden, dark emotions and memories. The truth is attitude is an important part of getting through the 4th step in a timely manner.

If you let emotions and fear bog you down, it becomes a far more highly charged, quicksand-like experience. But you *can* change the way you look at this step so you see it is a steppingstone toward relief and a better life ... which will allow you to move through it in a timely way.

Further, if this is your first 4th step, you don't have to suffer angst that you haven't uncovered every single issue of resentment, fear, sexual conduct issues, and other harms because, if you stay in recovery, you will probably do more than one 4th Step inventory, and eventually, you will do a daily mini-4th step once you reach Step 10 ("Continued to take personal inventory and when we were wrong promptly admitted it.").

Just for Today: Remember that each time you use this tool, it gets easier. Look at Step 4 as practice for living each day conscientiously in Recovery.

April 4 — A Prosperous Life

In recovery, we learn that prosperity is not always measured by income. For instance, we might need a new computer and someone gives us a spare one or we fall in love with a hobby that is inexpensive or free, but fills us with joy. As we proceed on the path of recovery, we discover that we don't have to feel inferior to others because of money or status.

Through working a diligent program, people are able to find good paying jobs, create loving relationships, and see their income rise. When we learn that we have enough, fear, worry and resentment fall away. Debt disappears!

For some of us, excess means trouble, whether it's money, material things, or emotions. Because of recovery, we can redefine "prosperity." Prosperity is not about cash. We can have abundance in our spiritual program, creativity, relationships, and service.

Just for Today: If you are in self-pity about your financial situation or job, think of ways you are prosperous and fulfilled that have nothing to do with money.

April 5 — Relief of Fear

On page 84, the Big Book promises that "fear of people and of economic insecurity will leave us." Nowhere does the Big Book say that we will not experience economic insecurity … just that we won't fear it. In D.A., we know that if the worst happens, we are armed with tools to keep us steadily walking through whatever we must face one day at a time. When we work our program, fear of people is removed because we are not so much in conflict with others. We are no longer hiding from creditors and do our best to pay off any debt we may have. We know that we are not our debt and do not let others make us feel less than because of it. When we make a mistake, we learn to take ownership of it as soon as possible and make amends when necessary for our part, without shame. If we haven't wronged or deceived others, it's a good day, and we don't have to fear retribution. And even if someone does cause us harm, we have tools to help us get right-minded about it. Because we do our best to live honestly and in integrity, we don't have to fear people. We may not always get them to do what we want, but we are not constantly trying to manipulate them either.

Just for Today: Can you feel the relief of living with less fear that recovery brings?

April 6 — The Second Arrow

The Serenity prayer tells us to accept the things we cannot change. Death is a thing we cannot change. Time passing is a thing we cannot change (though we can choose to spend it wisely). Acceptance is the opposite of fear. Acceptance has a relaxing quality to it, whereas fear escalates.

Being in the present moment just feels better ... at least when the present moment is pleasant. But even when it isn't, we can bear discomfort for just this one moment and then the next, and the next, knowing that all things pass.

Fear and resentment go hand-in-hand. Both are in our mind. Resentment is about reliving a past event and fear is usually about the future, though we can certainly work ourselves up reliving a fearful event.

Just as we don't romance spending anymore, instead choosing to move our mind to something else when the thought first enters, when fear blankets us, we can come out from under the covers by reminding ourselves that all is well in this moment and bringing ourselves back to the present.

Just for Today: We cannot prevent the first arrow of a disturbing thought from striking us, but we can choose not to shoot ourselves with a second.

April 7 — Outreach Etiquette

Outreach calls are an integral part of our recovery, allowing us to connect on a personal level with fellow compulsive debtors and spenders while providing us with an opportunity to give service. Whether making or receiving outreach calls, we follow rules of common courtesy. When we make a call, instead of immediately launching in with what we'd like to talk about, we first ask if this is a good time for the person to speak with us. When receiving a call, if we only have a moment, we let the caller know up-front so that we don't unintentionally cause hurt feelings by abruptly ending the call without warning. For the same reason, we do not answer call waiting unless there is an important reason to do so. We are mindful of the time, generally keeping our outreach calls to 15 minutes. And if we don't know the other person, we may want to use some discretion when revealing intimate information. While we need to find solidarity and support, it takes time to develop a trusting relationship. Most importantly, we try always to allow the other person to share as well, doing our best to be an active listener. Even if we are new to the program, we can be a source of comfort for another recovering compulsive debtor.

Just for Today: We are respectful of members of our fellowship at meetings and on the phone.

April 8   Keep Moving

The key is not to let emotions STOP you from moving forward and through working Step 4. As you can see from the Big Book's example on page 65, you *can* move quickly through this process and still be thorough by writing your 4th Step using phrases and brief notes as a springboard for your 5th Step discussion with your sponsor.

Further, while the Big Book states that we do a fearless and thorough inventory, that doesn't mean you can't move on if you haven't gotten every single thing down on paper. If you live a recovery life, you will not only have another opportunity to do a formal 4th step, but, again, you will eventually get to Step 10 ("Continued to take personal inventory and when we were wrong promptly admitted it.") where you may remember what you now forgot.

It may be a good idea to set a date with your sponsor for your 5th step to give you a deadline for completing the 4th step. Too many members become mired in this step and never move past it. It is not here to stop you, but to propel you forward into a deeper level of recovery.

Just for Today: If you are working on your 4th Step, read page 65 of the Big Book. Set up a schedule for working on your 4th Step on a regular basis, even for just a few minutes each day.

April 9 — Gotta Have 'Em

A spending plan must, by necessity, include categories, but how detailed and specific is really a personal preference. For instance, one member may need to track spending for food groceries separate from house supplies, such as soap and toilet paper. Others find that too detailed and lump everything purchased at a grocery store into one category. We can experiment with more or less detail until we find the level that works for us to maintain clarity in our spending. For instance, a member once said that she spent so much time trying to be sure she was allocating spending to the exact right category that she was ready to leave the program. Her answer was to make bigger bucket categories. While she has a house category where she tracks her mortgage and utilities, her food, gas, restaurants, household supplies, etc., are all lumped into one big category called Consumables. This system has really worked for her, but would create vagueness for others. There is no hard and fast rule about categories and subcategories ... except that you need some!

Just for Today: Are your spending plan categories working to enhance your recovery?

April 10 — Crucial 4th Step Tips

Do each column of your 4th Step one at a time. Please do not go across the sheet. In other words, first, list all the people, places, principles that have you resentful or riled up. Don't list one and then go to the next column to write about what happened to make you riled up. This has been universally accepted as the easiest and least painful way to work your 4th step.

As someone suggested, think about this process like a car mechanic fixing a car. No need to get overly emotional when dredging up the past. It's ok to be dispassionate. Doing a thorough inventory doesn't need to cause emotional angst.

Don't procrastinate. Get started on it as soon as possible. There is nothing to be gained by waiting once you have done Steps 1-3. The sooner you start, the sooner you will find relief as everyone does who moves on to the rest of the steps.

Just for Today: If you need some encouragement to help you move through Step 4, read the Promises of Debtors Anonymous.

April 11 — Making Outreach Calls

Like it or not, making outreach calls on a regular basis is a fire drill for when you are in trouble. Many addicts are isolators. Though we may be highly social when we can act like the big spender with others, we may not be as gregarious when it comes to revealing the truth about ourselves in recovery. But the essence of all 12 Step programs is that we share out experience, strength, and hope with each other in order to recover.

Some of us work a D.A. program where we are expected to make a daily outreach call and to talk about ourselves as part of the conversation. How can we do this with virtual strangers? No one expects you to pour out your entire life story to someone you've only just met on the phone. However, if you remember that we share a common problem and that it is by doing service that we recover, it may become easier to open up. In a sense, we are not strangers at all. Each of us is here because we cannot handle money soberly. When you hear someone share something that resonates with your own patterns of behavior at a meeting, that would be a good person to contact. Great friendships that go far beyond the rooms of D.A. have grown out of just such outreach calls.

Just for Today: Make an outreach call.

April 12   Generosity, Not Grandiosity

In recovery, we learn the difference between generosity and grandiosity. The Merriam Webster online dictionary first defines generosity as "the quality of being kind, understanding, and not selfish" and then as "willingness to give money and other valuable things to others." Nowhere does it say that generosity includes giving away other peoples' money, which is what credit cards allowed us to do. Grandiosity is defined as "seeming to be impressive or intended to be impressive but not really possible or practical." In other words, grandiosity is living with flair, but in a way that is not honest and true to ourselves.

Fixing your uncle's computer, helping to pack up your best friend's garage, and giving your niece a box of clothing your child has outgrown are examples of generosity that costs us nothing but saves our loved ones financially. On the other hand, sponsoring, being the time-keeper at a meeting, and answering an outreach call are acts of service that are priceless.

Just for Today: We no longer have to define our generosity by how much money we throw around at restaurants or how expensive a gift we buy.

April 13 — Yes, Not Now, or Something Better

This phrase captures the spirit of acceptance and a sober point of view. When we want something to manifest in our life, such as a new job, we take the next right action but turn the results over to our Higher Power. "Yes" means that we get the job we interviewed for. "Not now" is the answer if someone else was hired. But unlike "no" or "never," "not now" means that a future opportunity will better suit us, which is where we find the "something better."

We all love "yes" because we get what we want immediately. "Not now" is where we feel the pain of delay and rejection, and it may trigger a visceral reaction akin to "it's not fair." Despite that, we can choose recovery and sit with the discomfort as we continue to pursue our goal.

"Something better" is where we live when we find ourselves disappointingly deprived of what we want, such as a job, a date, or a house. Many of us can attest to the miraculous power of "something better." When we become willing to let go of what we cannot have, we can then open ourselves to what may come, which may well be "something better."

Just for Today: Remember that acceptance includes letting go.

April 14 — Accumulation

In the vagueness of our compulsive debting and spending, we may have accumulated a lot of "stuff." Sometimes, we even have multiples of the same item. Too often, we have never even worn, read, or used the clothing, books, or art supplies we possess. Some of us continue to collect more and more without using what we have. Becoming conscious of this behavior can be part of our recovery process. We can also work to let go of what we no longer need without fear. In recovery, some of us find relief in donating or giving away what we have accumulated in the wreckage of our past. But if we are impulsive in our effort, it may backfire and cause resentment. Others of us continue to be fearful of letting go of something we might need, and live with the boxes, bags, or storage units of unused merchandise. Accumulation *can* weigh on us, emotionally, physically, and spiritually. But we want to be mindful of why we are letting go of what we have when we do so. There is a delicate balance in this spiritual practice. By consciously getting rid of what you don't use, you make room for something new to come into your life, and by using what you do have, you are choosing to live more consciously.

Just for Today: Are you willing to use what you have before acquiring more?

April 15 — Income Tax Day

Many people dread April 15th because it is the day they have to pay the piper. For others, they resent the time and effort they need to expend figuring out their taxes. But in recovery, this is a day we can celebrate if we have sent in our tax forms on time. For those who end up paying tax, it is a testimony to their clarity around finances and the fact that they earned enough money to participate in paying dues. For those who get a refund, this is a celebration not only for the obvious reason, but because they were clear enough to keep track of items that would offset any tax they might owe.

In years past, many of us either blew off the deadline or kept no records to aid us in reducing our tax liability. When we first come into D.A., we do have to clean up the wreckage of our past, which, for many of us, includes catching up with our income taxes. It can appear to be a scary proposition, but many happily recovering member of D.A. have come through the process far stronger and more committed to their recovery.

Just for Today: Have you completed your taxes?

April 16 — Don't Believe Everything You Think

Just because we're in recovery doesn't mean our thinking is always right. Referring to the notion that our thoughts are always inspired, page 87 of the Big Book states, "We might pay for this presumption in all sorts of absurd actions and ideas." This is why we cannot work our program alone, and we need more than just a sponsor to guide us on this path. We need the support and suggestions of our PRG team, meetings, and network to help us through difficult choices and temptations. Money is a particularly challenging foe when it comes to inspired thinking.

We might believe that it is our destiny to change careers, begin health treatments, buy a house, or get a dog when our financial circumstances are clearly showing us that we cannot afford to do so at this time. Our UN-inspired thinking may make us desperate because we believe the intensity of the desire is our Higher Power's will for us, but the vision we think is inspired is really our disease trying to outwit us and convince us there is no choice but to debt.

Just for Today: If your seemingly inspired thought means bankrupting yourself or debting, pause and reach out for help to discern the truth of the situation.

April 17   Love and Fear

"If it is true that there are only two main emotions in life, love and fear, then all that we don't do out of love we are doing out of fear." (Page 69, "Drop the Rock.") This means that we have two choices in any situation. And fear doesn't have to win out just because it's louder. Fear cloaks itself in envy, anger, frustration, shame, greed, jealousy, and resentment, trying to convince us that the world will end if we don't get our way, and that there isn't enough for everyone. Love is a soothing balm for our soul, allowing our adrenalized selves to let go of grasping. Love and fear are not esoteric principles, but actions we take in every moment. We let someone go ahead of us in traffic. That is kindness, a form of love. We cut someone off in traffic. That is greed, a feeling that we must win, that our time and needs come first, which is all just fear of losing our place. Each moment we have a choice about the next action to take. We can let fear drive the bus or we can pause when inflamed and take no action until we come back to our senses. Fear tries to shove us over the cliff, hoping we will act on fiery emotions. Love lets us land on a soft cushion, providing a soothing balm for our emotions.

Just for Today: We can always choose the path of the heart, which allows for kindness, even in the face of fear.

April 18 — Deprivation or Justification

In recovery, we are told that we do not live in deprivation. But some of us confuse that idea with justifying discretionary purchases we cannot afford. Is it deprivation if we cannot afford to go to a concert or meditation retreat or another special event this month? Or is that just living life on life's terms? Yes, it's true that we first ensure that we have enough money for food, housing, clothing essentials, and other such areas of our life, before we pay our creditors. And unlike a budget, we also plan for some of our wants as well before doing so. But, we must also learn to balance our spending plan so we don't deprive ourselves in essential categories just to feed the beast of our binge categories. And we don't put all our discretionary money into certain categories (for instance art supplies or clothing) when we know that we may also want to spend on other discretionary items (such as buying books and going to the movies). When we live in such a balanced way, we don't need to regularly raid some categories to make up for the shortfall by overfunding others.

Just for Today: We can remember that "you can't always get what you want," are not just the lyrics to a song. It's the truth about recovery from compulsive debting and spending.

April 19   Living in the Next Month

For some D.A. members, "living in the next month" has been a game-changer. We do this by using this month's income to fund next month's spending. For example, if you are paid on the 1st and 15th of April, when you get your paychecks, you use the money to plan your May spending.

To start this process, you have to accumulate enough money, either from savings, a windfall, or in a category, to get through a full month without spending the money you earn. Even if you have to slowly save up that one month's pay, it has been worth it for many D.A. members to experience the profound relief "living in the next month" brings.

Imagine not having to dig through the sofa for change so you can buy food the day before your next paycheck arrives. Imagine that you have all the money for the month available on the first of the month, instead of having it look great on paper, but not in real-time cash flow. This system works for people who receive a regular paycheck and especially well as for freelancers who are not paid on a regular basis.

Just for Today: Think about saving toward living in the next month.

April 20 — Type A or Type B

In D.A., the only requirement for membership is a desire to stop debting. However, regarding our use of money and what causes people to come into program, we are generally either people who cannot stop spending (often out of fear of not having enough) or people who cannot bear to spend (often out of fear of not having enough).

Those in either category may have no debt at all, yet the program of Debtors Anonymous can be just as miraculous for them as for those of us with debt. A compulsive spender without debt is just a debtor who hasn't run out of money yet. As for those who are spending anorexic, the pain is just as excruciating as for the compulsive spender. But in the end, it doesn't matter why you came in because we share a common problem, which is that we are out of control with money in some fashion and for either type, the solution is the same.

Just for Today: Do you accept anyone who says he or she is a member without judgment about how his or her addiction manifests?

April 21 — Surrender

To most of us, the idea of surrender is quite negative, but in reality, it is actually a companion to relaxation. The Merriam-Webster online dictionary defines surrender as agreeing "to stop fighting, hiding, resisting, etc., because you know that you will not win or succeed." Isn't this what happens when we finally come into D.A. having hit bottom?

We can extend this philosophy into many areas of our life. When faced with physical or emotional pain, or not getting our way, if we fight it, our situation usually worsens because we become tense and get worked up. What would happen if we surrendered instead of resisted? We might find that our pain lessens and our expectations release. During meditation, we have many opportunities to practice surrender in a safe environment. For instance, if you have a headache, as you sit in the quiet of your surroundings, try to melt into the center of the pain instead of tightening up in resistance.

If you hit brick walls in your efforts to accomplish a goal, instead of lashing out in frustration, slow your breathing down and sit quietly, surrendering to the truth of the moment, deliberately softening into the place of disturbance, allowing it to wash over you instead of bite you.

Just for Today: Practice surrender into pain.

April 22   Embrace Your Spending Plan

Our spending plan is an integral component in our recovery from compulsive debting and spending. If you have a spending plan, trust it and live by it. If you don't yet have a spending plan, work on getting one with a PRG team.

Living by our spending plan means that we stay within the allotted amounts in our categories unless we have a PRG or clear any changes with our sponsor. If your spending plan is out of balance or you feel that you are manipulating it, have a PRG to help you revise it. In fact having an annual PRG review of your spending plan is a great idea.

The spending plan is the tool by which we live in balance with money on a physical level and can provide much-needed relief if we can accept the limitations it creates as well as the freedom it provides.

Just for Today: Do you spend within the framework of your spending plan's categories?

April 23 — Gift Giving

Gift giving is often an area where our ego kicks in. Prior to recovery, many of us gave presents that far exceeded what we could afford to spend on them. We loved giving an extravagant gift or at least making sure our gift is as nice (meaning expensive) as everyone else's. In recovery, we learn balance in gift giving. In the beginning, some of us may not be able to afford to give gifts at all. Even when we can do so, we may still be faced with difficult choices. For instance, if an unexpected life event occurs, such as a relative's hospitalization, we might not be able to give a gift because our accruing funds are being saved for other scheduled events. The boundaries around gift giving can be an area that causes us tremendous pain and feelings of humiliation if we were big spenders in the past. The first few years in recovery parents may have an especially hard time when their children's birthdays or holidays come around. We can develop creative ways to give when we don't have a lot of money. For instance, for my son's 21st birthday, I wrote and had printed a book about our lives together. This was far more meaningful to him than another bright and shiny object.

Just for Today: Let us remember that money doesn't equal love.

April 24 — Vagueness Is Our Enemy

There are few things as dangerous to our recovery as vagueness around money. Vagueness can cause us to over- or under-estimate need in an area, resulting in a domino effect in our categories, which can lead to debting. For instance, when we first get into recovery, we may not know how to save for annual or quarterly bills, such as car registration or property taxes. A simple solution is to divide the total due by the number of months between payments. If our car registration is $100 a year, we divide by 12, which equals $8.33/month. It's best to increase by a few pennies to cover a shortfall that may occur with the change. In this case, we might then save $8.40/month. For a quarterly bill, divide by the total per quarter by three. Apportioning our spending in this way may appear to create more limits on discretionary spending if we are used to scrambling at the last minute to pay. But that is just an illusion. We can continue to pretend that we have more money by ignoring future bills until they arrive, but it is only by dividing future bills into small monthly accruals that we can breathe easier when payments are due.

Just for Today: Do you want to live in reality or fantasy?

April 25 — Dealing with Obsession

How can we deal with obsession, that breathless, heart-pounding, adrenaline pumping feeling that we will *die* if we don't buy what we want *now*? Obsession is the driving characteristic of compulsive debting and spending. For one thing, we can learn to take the wind out of obsession's sails by pausing for at least 24 hours (or longer) before making purchases when we are drowning in that adrenalized feeling. We think that the only way to quiet the pain is to make the purchase, but that is not true. Though we believe that the pain of desire is endless, waiting always calms those feelings eventually. We can talk to our sponsor, PRG team, and network when enveloped by obsession. They can often calm us down and provide a different way to look at the situation. Meditation (as suggested in Step 11) gives us practice with sitting in discomfort, instead of fighting it, so we learn that we will not die from those feelings. We can also pray for the courage to bear the discomfort until comfort comes. And finally, if we can't afford the object of our obsession today, we can remind ourselves that we can do so once we have the funds. In the meantime, we can be grateful for our willingness to stay sober with money.

Just for Today: In recovery, we have many tools to help us deal with obsession sanely.

April 26   Feeling Our Pain

A meditation teacher once said, "We need to belly up to our own suffering and feel it." How challenging that is. We want to be comfortable. We don't want to hurt. But our program of recovery is about accepting reality ... life on life's terms. And those terms are sometimes painful.

In order to stay sober with money, we must face the fact that we can't always have what we want the moment we want it. In fact, sometimes, the truth is that we can't have what we want at all.

When this happens, we may rail against the facts, rebelling against our sponsors and PRG teams, whose role it is to help us accept what we cannot change while guiding us to the actions we can take to change the things we can. But they cannot keep us from feeling the pain of hitting the wall when we want something that we just cannot have today.

This is where the rubber meets the road in recovery. When we are faced with "no," we can choose to escape into the fantasy that no means yes and revert to our old ways ... or we can stay the course on the path of recovery, knowing that eventually, the painful feelings will pass.

Just for Today: Do you believe that allowing yourself to feel the pain of not getting what you want is the best way to heal from it?

April 27   A Day Off

We have to accept the fact that even in recovery, we may experience emotions around money, whether it's spending it, saving it, or having to pick and choose what we buy. But working our program can help us change from suffering to acceptance around it. In recovery, we may actually find more peace in not spending than we do in the temporary "ahhhhhhhhh" of buying something. We learn to enjoy, and even choose, days where don't spend any money. Some of us may feel a great calm on those days, even a sense of relief. Others of us, on days of no spending, find that all the stuff we want to buy continues wandering around in our mind, but we become empowered by choosing to refrain from taking action, and we *can* feel gratefully released from the yearning to buy any of those items just for today. Just as taking a day for meditative reflection is a spiritual practice, so too can choosing to refrain from discretionary spending for 24 hours. This powerful practice gives us the opportunity to be grateful for what we have without painfully yearning for what we don't.

Just for Today: Choose to take a day off from spending any money.

April 28 — Sitting with Money

For many compulsive debtors, money burns a hole in their pocket, so learning how to sit with this discomfort is one of the first challenges they face. The irony is that the longer we are sober with money, the more we are bound to accumulate, which can make some of us feel an overwhelming itch to spend. For members with health issues or those who have a career change in mind, the temptation to use our retirement savings or prudent reserve can be enormous. After all, we may think, this is not debting. But if we spend down our retirement savings or prudent reserve, we are far more at risk of debting if a crisis comes along. That is why it is better to save within specific categories for our daily needs and wants. But what do we do about the yearning to spend our retirement savings or prudent reserve on our visions or our health? The only answer is a spiritual one. We use the tools of recovery to shift our thinking into acceptance that we save in specific categories for our dreams and non-emergency medical treatments instead of raiding our retirement savings or prudent reserve to accomplish such discretionary goals.

Just for Today: Do you believe that a balanced financial life means that we save for our future as well as our dreams?

April 29 — Analysis Paralysis

In recovery, we may actually find it hard to spend money for discretionary items because the sky is no longer the limit. We learn how to research before making purchases for big ticket items like cars or computers. Often, we find ourselves paralyzed by the sheer volume of information available to us. It can be helpful to limit our selection by company or model early in the process so as not to experience option paralysis. When we live by our categories, we live within boundaries. We want to do our best to sure that we make the "perfect" decision. The problem is that there are no guarantees. It's all about choices. Once we have made a selection, eventually we must cross the Rubicon. We can continue reading reviews endlessly, but at some point, it becomes pointless. If we are living within our means, there is no wrong decision. There are mistakes, and we can learn from them. And while we don't make a practice of returning items we buy, it is ok to return a purchase that isn't what we want or need. It's best to check the return policy of the store prior to buying the item to be sure you can do so.

Just for Today: Can you accept that spending decisions are choices, understanding that there are no guarantees?

April 30   Self-Knowledge *Can* Avail Something

While the Big Book says that simply understanding why you do what you do will not make you sober (in our case, with money), it's also true that for those in recovery from compulsive debting self-knowledge can help us move forward on our path. By working Step 11, which suggests daily prayer and meditation, we gain clarity about our triggers and how better to handle them, and learn how to discern whether the decisions before us are based on intuition or just obsession, fear, or anxiety.

We are asked to take time each day to speak to our Higher Power and listen for guidance. As with all things, including sobriety, it takes practice to improve our conscious contact with our Higher Power. If we only practice Step 11 sporadically, we will not improve our conscious contact and get to know the "still, small voice" of intuition within us. If we want to get to know who we are in recovery, we must be willing to sit in silence daily instead of racing through life in an effort to distract ourselves from self-knowledge.

Just for Today: Are you willing to practice prayer and meditation today?

May 1 — First of the Month Frenzy

The first of the month is often a day filled with lots of spending for those who must buy groceries, household items, and pay bills. It is often tight getting through that last week of the previous month abstinently in areas such as food and household goods. But for some of us, the first of the month also means our binge categories are replenished, which may tweak us weeks before the month ends if we have used up all the previous month's money in that category early on.

Unlike those in recovery from alcohol, we must deal with our drug of choice daily, or nearly so. That means that we will eventually have to learn how to purchase items in our binge category soberly. For some of us, this is one of the most challenging aspects of our recovery.

Dealing with this situation sanely month after month may mean dividing up our purchases throughout the month or at least waiting a few days into the month before spending the money in those categories. On a spiritual level, it means increasing gratitude and practicing patience. Step 11, prayer and meditation can help us suffer less waiting for the first of each month.

Just for Today: Can you wait 24 hours before spending money in categories that "tweak" you?

May 2 — Admitting to Our HP

Step 5 states that "we admitted to God, to ourselves, and to another human being the exact nature of our wrongs." Once my inventory was complete, I realized that writing it all down *was* the admission of the exact nature of my wrongs to my Higher Power and to myself! There was no other action I had to take on that front if I had been rigorously honest in completing my inventory.

There was no turning back ... thank goodness. Well, there was no turning back if I expected to be released from the hold my thoughts had on me as well as the guilt, shame, and remorse I experienced over my part in resentments, fears, sexual behavior, etc. As the Big Book says on page 59, "Half measures availed us nothing. We stood at the turning point. We asked His protection and care with complete abandon. Here are the steps we took, which are suggested as a program of recovery…"

And lo and behold, just by completing the writing of your 4th Step, you will find yourself smack in the middle of Step 5!

Just for Today: Enjoy the relief of that moment when you know you have done your best on your 4th Step, remembering imperfection is part of the human condition and not an indication of lack of willingness.

May 3   Just Do It!

Now that you've finished your 4th Step, all that's left is to admit these wrongs to another person. How terrifying, right? The very idea of stating the truth out loud to another person might make you hyperventilate or cause you bone-chilling angst. Still, if I can give you one suggestion, it is not to delay giving away your Fourth Step. Whatever is freaking you out in your Fourth Step will only grow larger, hairier, toothier, and meaner the longer you wait. Find someone immediately and get it over with

In nearly 30 years working multiple 12 Step programs, I have never come across a single person who did not feel a profound sense of relief and experience tremendous spiritual growth as a result of completing Steps 4 and 5.

Not to minimize whatever harm you may have caused, but unless you have dismembered people for fun (in which case, you will need far more than a 4th and 5th Step to help you), once you have stated your wrongs out loud, you will realize how your mind has blown them up far bigger than they actually were.

Just for Today: You may find that the grudge you have held for so long simply dissolves along with the words that evaporate after you speak about it.

May 4 — Intuition

Page 84 of the Big Book promises that "we will intuitively know how to handle situations which used to baffle us." Intuition is tricky. Sometimes we may think we're acting out of intuition, but it's just willfulness or craving in disguise. Being in recovery doesn't mean we don't make mistakes. It's *learning* from our mistakes that is key, along with understanding that we don't have to make decisions on our own. In recovery life, there are four parts to intuitions: praying for guidance; meditating for answers; talking to trusted people in our network to get feedback; waiting. (Whenever possible, we pause for at least 24 hours or more to see how we feel over time.) We begin to understand that desire is not the same as craving. Craving is a rush. Desire is a preference.

In recovery, we do not act impulsively. First, we learn to do this with our spending, and then we find ourselves behaving this way in other areas of our life. Sometimes, we still need to step into experiences to determine if they are a good idea or not. But we don't have to beat ourselves up if we make a mistake. Progress is that we no longer jump in without thinking.

Just for Today: Try this prayer for decision-making: Higher Power, if it is your will, increase my desire. If it is not your will, decrease my desire.

May 5   Funding Our Contingency

It is suggested that we create a category for emergencies, such as an unexpected house, medical, or car repair that exceeds the amount we may have saved in categories specific to these events. This Contingency category is separate from our main Savings category, which is intended for long-term goals, such as retirement. When determining how much to keep in our Contingency category, we can turn to our PRG team, sponsor, and network for help. We don't want to overfund it, keeping it simply as a slush fund. But we want to ensure that the minimum is sufficient based on our life circumstances. For instance, a single person may work to keep $1,000 available, but a single mother of two may want to keep $3,000. If we are new to D.A., the whole idea of a Contingency fund may seem outlandish when we are just learning how to live within our means and discovering that it is tight all the way around, with little to no money available for savings, much less a Contingency category. But we can aspire to this important self-care approach. And while we don't sacrifice our needs to accrue these funds, we also stay mindful of the importance of having a way to handle emergencies without debting.

Just for Today: Create a Contingency category in your spending plan if you don't yet have one.

May 6 — Strong Sponsorship

Sponsorship is a vital service in D.A.. However, it is not enough to take on a sponsee. We must also be mindful of the tremendous responsibility inherent in this role. Yes, we have agreed to share our experience, strength, and hope with another D.A. member to help them on their recovery path. But how we do this is the key to successful sponsorship. A responsible sponsor is available for the sponsee's call at the agreed-upon time. There is little more demoralizing to a new member than hopefully dialing that number, only to reach voice mail. This type of disappointment holds true for members at any stage of their recovery. While an emergency may come up from time to time, if we agree to sponsor, we need to be available when we say we will. Strong sponsors share their experience, strength, and hope. They do not give advice. But when asked, they may make suggestions based on their own experience. Strong sponsors do not act as relationship, financial, or career counselors. Strong sponsors are active listeners. They do not multi-task during their sponsee calls. Strong sponsors lay out the guidelines for how they work their program as a roadmap for the sponsee, but they release a sponsee with kindness if a sponsee's actions compromise their own program.

Just for Today: Are you a strong sponsor?

May 7 — Who Am I?

D.A. is a program that gets to the core of how we see ourselves in relation to the world. Compulsive debting and spending tend to be social addictions. We pay for the big dinner, buy the extravagant present, wear the right clothes. Our addiction is very much about our idea of how the world sees us.

Recovery from this addiction is about seeing ourselves more right-sized, caring less about form and more about substance. We move from the external to the internal, from the material to the spiritual. We first begin to make this transition by learning to live within our means. Though this seems to be just a mundane aspect of recovery, it is actually a highly spiritual practice.

When we live within our means in a sober manner, we learn lessons about humility, ego, anger, integrity, resentment, jealousy, longing, creativity, sharing, giving, acceptance, and much more. We begin to see who we really are, rather than the image we presented to the world. In areas such as gift giving, living within our means inspires innovation and creativity when we can't spend as we used to, leading us to learn that the best gifts of all are freely given from the heart, not the pocketbook.

Just for Today: Do you know who you are?

May 8   One Step Back

Recovery doesn't follow a straight trajectory. Spiritual lessons are most often gained from pain, not pleasure. It is when our world is shaken up that we grow most deeply. There was once a woman who, prior to recovery, made some poor life choices and caused pain to others because of those decisions. Once sober, she desperately sought relief from the suffering she experienced from the lingering effects of the wreckage of her past. Finally, she sought refuge in a meditation retreat. While there, she asked the teacher why she continued to suffer so deeply when she was doing her best to be a "spiritual person." His response was that "first, you must be good." This simple message tells us that sobriety, alone, is not enough. We must also shift our focus from how we can make ourselves feel better to how we can make things right. Eliminating self-centeredness and taking responsibility for our actions, both past and present is a long-term proposition that involves peeling away layers of denial. It is just when you think you have made great progress that you may suddenly find the rug pulled out from under you. It is this dance that moves us forward on the path of recovery, not a straight-forward march.

Just for Today: Do you live in self-pity or service?

May 9 — Customer Service

We have many opportunities to practice patience and acceptance as we walk through our day. Speaking with customer service representatives when we have a problem can be especially fertile ground for working on our character defects. Prior to making the call, we can take a moment to say the Serenity prayer, reminding ourselves that the results are out of our hands. As we wait on hold, we can note that the person with whom we speak is simply doing his job to the best of his ability. If all doesn't go as we would like, practicing calm in the face of resistance can be a huge victory in our recovery journey. We don't have to argue with the person on the other end of the phone. And we can certainly escalate the situation if we feel that will be useful. But we can do this with grace and dignity. This behavior can be extended to the way that we deal with our creditors. If we have debt, it is true that we owe them money and it may be true that we cannot make even a minimum payment, but neither of those facts makes us "bad" people ... nor does it mean we have to behave in ways we will later regret because we are embarrassed about it.

Just for Today: Use customer service and creditor interactions as an opportunity to work your program.

May 10 — Deprivation Mentality

Some D.A. members experience excruciating difficulty spending money for need and wants, even if the money is available. We are gently nudged to spend the money in our categories. Otherwise, some people will use discretionary categories as a way to hoard money. For instance, someone may not buy clothing for work when his wardrobe is threadbare or insist on going to the laundromat instead of buying a new washing machine, despite the fact that the associated categories continue to accrue. Sometimes the fear is that once the door is opened, their spending will spiral out of control, so they continue to hold on to every penny for dear life.

Miracles happen for D.A. members who overcome their fear, and trust that there is enough and that they can spend their money soberly. We have seen members whose lives have blossomed after taking the leap of faith to follow their PRG team's direction, and watched as abundance followed in both work and relationships when they spent according to their spending plan.

Just for Today: Am I willing to trust my spending plan?

May 11 — Good Decisions

A good life is made up of a series of good decisions. When we were active in our addiction, we may have bemoaned our fate, feeling powerless over the state of our lives. However, if we reviewed the events that led us to where we are now, we could usually see where a poor decision led to the dominoes falling as they did.

Impulsive action more often leads to poor decision-making than measured consideration and patience. Compulsive debting and spending is often associated with an inability to delay gratification, which can lead to impulse buying. That is why we learn to recognize obsession so we can choose to pause rather than react.

In recovery, we learn to take responsibility for our actions and we are given tools to help us make better choices. Once we understand that obsession is just a bad decision waiting to happen cloaked in desperate desire, we learn to live with the painful feelings until they pass. We turn to the tools of phone call, prayer, and meditation to aid us in waiting for the grip of obsession to loosen before taking action.

Just for Today: Do you understand that good decisions are not based on momentary desires?

May 12   Creditors Do Not Come First

According to D.A. Tool #5 – Spending Plan, "The debt payment category guides us in making realistic payment arrangements without depriving ourselves." In other words, our needs come first. In D.A., you begin debt repayment only after our spending plan covers our basic needs and some of our wants. This doesn't mean that we buy a winter home in Hawaii or a red Ferrari and ignore our creditors. But if we pay our creditors at the expense of food and medical care, our spending plan and life are out of balance. With a "budget" philosophy, *any* discretionary spending is frowned upon. For instance, I include a monthly massage as part of my spending plan because it provides relief for a medical condition. My husband thinks it is a ridiculous luxury. Sometimes, I feel embarrassed about this choice. But when I talk to my sponsor and PRG, I get right-minded again. Thankfully, in program, we are surrounded by people who have gone before us and know that we are still entitled to a life despite having debt. Maybe we only have $5 in our entertainment category. But at least we have something. Otherwise, the ongoing deprivation will lead to binge spending and debting.

Just for Today: With the help of your sponsor, PRG team, and network, you can develop a sober spending plan.

May 13   Firm or Mean?

There is a difference between a sponsor who is firm and one who is mean. A firm sponsor does not bend his recovery to fit the whims of a sponsee. If a sponsee makes decisions that violate the foundations of the sponsor's recovery, he can explain why this is so. If the sponsee insists on having her way, a firm sponsor will lovingly tell her that she is welcome to do so, but he cannot continue sponsoring her as it will disturb his own program. A mean sponsor would tell the sponsee that she will lose her abstinence if she does what she wants rather than listening to the sponsor.

A mean sponsor will demean a sponsee who disagrees with her. A firm sponsor is willing to hear out the sponsee, but will not engage in argument.

A mean sponsor judges lifestyle choices of a sponsee and gives advice, rather than suggestions. A firm sponsor shares her experience, strength, and hope with a sponsee to guide him on his journey.

Just for Today: Remembering that our program is based on service, we try always to share our program in a loving way.

May 14   Family Support

If our parents or other family members habitually provided financial support when we were in trouble before we came into D.A., it can be challenging to say no to these "gifts" once we are in recovery. For some, the best choice may be to continue accepting the help. However, if you have come to see that the price you've paid for taking money from your family is that you are left feeling stuck, manipulated, angry, embarrassed, or humiliated, you may want to reconsider accepting future offers.

The fact is, there are few D.A. issues as complex as those involving our families and money. In the practical sense, it's not so easy to say no to money when we are in a difficult situation. But if accepting the money is fraught with expectations, then we may want to consider breaking the cycle, even if it's painful. As with all addictive behavior, if the pain of accepting a gift wrapped in control becomes worse than the pain we are avoiding by taking it, we will become willing to face the repercussions of saying no, reminding ourselves that we have a program of recovery and a network of support to help us deal with the situation.

Just for Today: Examine your motivations for accepting financial support from your family.

May 15 — Awareness vs. Planning

When we first come into D.A., we are told to write down every penny we spend in order to gain awareness about our spending patterns. But some members never proceed beyond this point. Unfortunately, awareness is not enough for a sober life around money. While writing down our numbers tells us what we spent at any given moment, doing so in a vacuum can allow us to continue spending recklessly. If we want to live in recovery around our spending, we must eventually develop and live by a spending plan. This tool gives us the big picture of where our money needs to go and the detail about how to get there. But it also means accepting spending limits. Living by a spending plan means that we can no longer blindly spend as we want, telling ourselves that we are solvent because we write our numbers down, while we continue to live on the edge or worse. Shifting from spending to planning is a huge step in recovery from compulsive debting and spending.

Just for Today: Writing down our numbers moves us from the darkness into the shadows of awareness. But living by a spending plan brings us into the light of clarity.

May 16   Fame Is Not a Feeling

There may be famous people who prance about making the most of their fame, but how many others end up dead due to drug overdoses or get divorce after divorce? If fame were a panacea, wouldn't it bring a sense of peace and satisfaction with it? Instead, fame, in the wrong hands, just brings a craving for more, more, more.

This is akin to the compulsive debtor who believes the delusion that just this one last purchase will bring the ultimate feeling of satisfaction, and when it doesn't, she keeps scratching that itch in its search. The big lie for compulsive debtors is that we will stop debting or spending once we have enough money or once we finally get whatever it is that is in front of our craving brain at the moment. In recovery, we learn that the "feel-good" feeling we seek is generated inside of us ... by our right efforts ... and not by what the world thinks of us or satisfying an urge to buy the next bright and shiny object.

Just for Today: For true compulsive debtors, there will never be enough, so we learn to live within our means instead of using money as a drug.

May 17 — Bigger Is Not Better

When we first come into recovery, it may seem that our life grows smaller when compared to the grandiose way we lived in our addiction, and in ways measured by our fame-craving, success-seeking society. But for many of us, the smaller our lives become (i.e., ego), the more opportunity we have to develop spiritually and creatively.

Where we once strove for worldly success and acclaim, we now develop a rich internal and spiritual life that fulfills us in ways far more profound and meaningful. We may still work toward achievement, but our focus becomes more balanced, and we bring service to others to the forefront. Whatever our financial situation, recovery brings us internal riches by following our heart in addition to our dreams. Achievement means something quite different to us now, and for many in recovery, being of service has replaced fame and acquisition as a goal.

Just for Today: Can you appreciate the glorious gifts of a "small" life?

May 18   You ARE an Artist

Many recovering debtors are artists, writers, or otherwise creatively talented. They often struggle with finding a way to support themselves through their art, and become despondent when they cannot do so because they have bought into the idea that "if you do what you love, the money will follow," which is unfortunately, not always the case. On top of that is the belief that if you don't get paid for your art, you cannot consider yourself an artist. So when a creative cannot make money on her art, she may stop doing the very work that feeds her soul, believing that it is not worth doing if there isn't money attached. But Maya Angelou was a cable-car conductor, JK Rowling was a secretary, and abstract painter Mark Rothco was an elementary school teacher. Does that mean that the work they produced when they had a day job doesn't count? Vincent Van Gogh only sold one painting during his lifetime. Surely he is an artist. The joy we feel when creating is in the process, not so much in the sale. In fact, when process becomes production, art often becomes just another day job.

Just for Today: What creative activity makes your heart sing? Whether or not you can earn money with the finished product, you will find riches beyond compare if you allow yourself the joy of engaging in the process.

May 19   Prosperity Isn't Always Cash

Nowhere in the Steps or literature does it say that we will become financially wealthy and successful because we are sober with money. What the D.A. literature does say in the promises that "we will begin to live a prosperous life, unencumbered by fear, worry, resentment, or debt." and that "we will recognize that there is enough; our resources will be generous and we will share them with others and with D.A.." The AA Big Book promises on page 84 that "fear of people and of economic insecurity may leave us."

Prosperity and abundance don't always take the form of cash and worldly success. In my own case, I am blessed with a great living situation that I could never have afforded on my own, a car to drive, and an abundance of creativity that I am now able to express in ways that I never previously imagined! In addition, I no longer debt and will have the balance of my original $33,000 debt paid off in less than two years.

Just for Today: In what ways do you experience abundance besides cash?

May 20   Having Money Before Spending It

A commitment not to debt means more than simply cutting up our credit cards. It also means that we don't spend money before receiving it. For instance, even if you know you will be getting paid next week, it's not unheard of for paychecks to be late. For that reason, we don't float checks or tell people to wait before cashing them. While it's true that checks can take some time to clear, a commitment to recovery is about staying honest. Therefore, we write checks when we know we have the funds to cover them. What about refunds on purchased items we return? An even exchange or cash back at the store is fine. But if the store will refund our debit card, that is another matter. If we want to be honest with our spending, we will wait until the refund has cleared our bank account. This philosophy is not meant as punishment. The point is that we are working on recovery from vagueness around money, which can lead to debting. It's not about keeping you from spending your money, but about ensuring that you continually practice spending only money you actually have.

Just for Today: By following the guidelines above, you will be developing the habit of living within your means.

May 21   Do What You Love and...

The slogan "do what you love and you'll never work a day" is a dangerous concept for those who are committed to living within their means. The truth is that when we don't have credit cards to fall back on, we may have to get or keep a job we dislike until we find something more suitable. We may not be able to throw ourselves into living our vision when we have bills to pay and children to support. Any small business owner, no matter how much they love their work, will admit that there are tasks they dislike but must engage in to keep their business running. Writers and artists often struggle with balancing the creative, administrative, and marketing sides of their business. Most sole proprietors cannot afford to hire someone to assist them, but those who are successful just bite the bullet and do the work, understanding that, as Thomas Edison said, "Genius is one percent inspiration, ninety-nine percent perspiration." The fact is that "doing what we love" may be something that we do after we come home from work. But if we take pride in the work we do, we can find joy in our daily life. And when we get an opportunity to pursue our dreams, we don't balk at the tasks that require perspiration.

Just for Today: Do your work with gratitude.

May 22 — Gratitude Makes Acceptance Easier

In one of the Big Book stories ("Acceptance was the Answer," the person stated that "acceptance is the answer to all my problems today." But how do we accept situations that really challenge us?

The key to acceptance is gratitude. When we search out the good in our lives despite the difficulties we face, it helps us to shift our focus and perspective.

The fact is that everyone has challenges in their lives and opportunities that are denied. At some point, everyone deals with calamity and tragedy. By making gratitude a habit, we have an anchor to turn to when the darkness envelops us, to remind us that all is not lost.

Gratitude is like a series of bookmarks placed at points along the continuum of our lives. All we have to do is flip through our mental pages and we can find solace in remembering all that has been given to us, which is a far better use of our time and energy than focusing on what we lack. Gratitude can also give us the courage and motivation to seek out that which we *can* change even within a situation we must accept.

Just for Today: Allow gratitude to lead you to serenity.

May 23 — Keep It Simple

"Keep it Simple" is not just a slogan. It can be a way of life that enhances recovery. The Steps help us clear away the "wreckage of our past," but we must also learn how to move from chaos to order, to simplify our lives, if we are to enjoy our recovery.

We learn ways to calm ourselves, to keep from having adrenaline constantly coursing through our bodies, by meditation and reaching out to our D.A. network in times of stress. We learn to make more measured decisions instead of reacting instantly and impulsively, enslaved to our cravings and obsessions.

Keeping it simple means that we don't over-extend ourselves, either financially or emotionally. We think about the long-term consequences of our actions, not just the immediate reward. We learn that over-extending ourselves can lead to exhaustion, which can, in turn, lead to impulse buying and poor decision-making. We keep our spending simple by creating clear boundaries around purchasing through the use of a spending plan.

Every choice we make about how to spend our time, money, and energy determines whether we keep it simple and make recovery easier to maintain.

Just for Today: How can you simplify your life?

May 24 — Balance

The D.A. program is about balance. D.A. doesn't say, yes, hurry up and pay your debts and in the meantime, eat cat food and don't get that big lump on your leg checked out by the doctor, and oh, no, how can you even *think* about going to the movies much less having cable TV?!

It's true that debt is the albatross around many recovering debtors' necks … until they have been in recovery long enough to see their debts paid off the D.A. way. The fact is that a slow and steady approach will ensure that one's debt will eventually be paid off while also enabling us to take care of our body, mind, and spirit's needs as well as some of their wants.

Just for Today: Are you willing to sit in the discomfort of balancing debt repayment with self-care?

May 25 — Together

If we have taken the first step, "We admitted we were powerless over debt—that our lives had become unmanageable," we are already on the path to recovery. And remember, we are not alone. There are members we can turn to for help who have faced and overcome financial adversity equal to, or worse than, ours. As the expression goes, "Together we can do what we can never do alone."

Just for Today: Are you willing to turn to another D.A. member in times of difficulty?

May 26   Financial Security

The Big Book promises on page 84 that "fear of people and of economic insecurity will leave us." Nowhere is it written that we will make a big pile of money. D.A.'s promise that "we will begin to live a prosperous life, unencumbered by fear, worry, resentment, or debt," doesn't tell us what prosperity will look like in our lives.

In D.A., financial security doesn't always come in the form of cash. While some of us initially thought that increasing our earnings was the singular meaning of prosperity, we soon discovered that financial security can come in all sorts of forms, for example, a partner lovingly paying more toward the bills when we cannot contribute, receiving disability when we cannot work, or a friend's offer of an extra computer to replace the one that broke. Our needs and wants can often be taken care of in ways that don't involve earned income. As we come to find financial catastrophe averted time and again by seeming acts of Providence, we gradually become less and less fearful of economic insecurity.

Just for Today: Remember that each day we work our program without incurring unsecured debt, we are led deeper into a prosperous life unencumbered by fear, worry, and resentment.

May 27   The Enemy of Creativity

Some of us believe we work best with a deadline. But for many, panic over time passing can keep us blocked and stuck, and ironically, increase our procrastination because of it. This is true not only of external deadlines, but for those we place on ourselves. It is the kind of fear that rises up when we feel that there isn't enough time to write the book or create the art or plan the trip because time is passing and it will take too long, so why bother to start. And then passion gets lost in fear of the future.

It took 13 years for Stephen King to write The Stand. Twelve years for Richard Linklater to make the movie, "Boyhood." Time will pass, whether we engage or not. Most likely Steve Jobs was in mid-project when he finally shed his mortal coat. Michael Jackson was about to launch his biggest tour.

We should heed the creative voices inside of us and let go of worrying about how it will all turn out. Because in the end, just by engaging in the process, we will feed our soul in ways that money cannot buy.

Just for Today: When it comes to creative endeavors, focus on the journey rather than the destination.

May 28 — Uselessness and Self-Pity

Page 84 of the Big Book promises "that feeling of uselessness and self-pity will disappear." That's a tall order, but we are far less likely to experience those emotions when we work our program. It's hard to feel useless when you are sponsoring and doing other service-related activities. Self-pity is not tolerated by many sponsors, who give us the antidote – gratitude. They say a grateful heart doesn't pick up.

Many of us use the tool of gratitude daily to remind us of all we have, no matter what we lack. While it is not an official tool, many of us find gratitude an invaluable enhancement to the quality of our recovery.

It is doubly important for newcomers to work with gratitude. Newcomers are at the lowest point ... having their problems without benefit of all our program has to offer yet. By teaching newcomers to use the tool of gratitude, they might find some early relief. We don't have to wait. We can establish the habit of writing daily gratitudes, and experiencing the relief this practice offers, from the moment we come into recovery.

Just for Today: Have you established a daily gratitude practice?

May 29 — All in the Family

Being in recovery may mean breaking old patterns and habits when it comes to accepting money from our family if doing so negatively affects our self-esteem. Though we may worry that we need the continuing financial support, we now have an abundance of resources, including the D.A. tools, a network, and a Higher Power, to help us if we choose to say no. We don't have to do this all at once; we can gradually work toward financial independence.

Working the Steps around these issues can give us a better understanding about our own motivations in accepting money from our family, and clarity about whether accepting such financial support is enhancing our recovery. A 4th Step can help us to determine if we are being manipulative in this area, and later Steps show us how to take responsibility if that is the case.

Just for Today: Recovery doesn't mean that we have to say no unconditionally to financial help from our family. But if we do accept a financial gift, Recovery teaches us how to do so with integrity and good feeling.

May 30 — Saving the World

The Talmud, a book of Jewish law, states, "And whoever saves a life, it is considered as if he saved an entire world." When we do service in our program, we may not realize how important it is because it doesn't reach millions. But to the individual who has gratefully benefited from our efforts, it makes no difference how many other people have been helped.

When we work the Steps, we see the truth about our lives. Many of us suffered from grandiose thinking and big living that was completely out of proportion to reality. In recovery, we learn to see ourselves more right-sized, becoming humble in the process. We are then able to turn our focus toward a life of service, sharing our experience, strength, and hope with other suffering compulsive debtors.

Service has a cascading effect. To the compulsive debtor you help by reaching out, sponsoring, being on a PRG, or sharing at a meeting, the service you give is life-saving. By extension, the family of that person and anyone whose life she touches benefits by the recovery that she may now embrace.

Just for Today: Do you appreciate the importance of service?

May 31 — Integrity

Integrity is a quality that includes fairness, honesty, and a commitment to ethical behavior. One way we develop integrity is by learning to take responsibility for our part in a conflict instead of instinctively blaming others for our difficulties. In the past, ruminating on what others have done to us was a way of staying stuck and sick. This is no more than a manipulative tactic on the part of our addiction; an attempt to drive us to blot out the pain of our "pitiful" situation by acting out with money.

Stepping up to own our behavior instead of focusing on what others did wrong is character building. And the payoff is that we live with increased serenity and peace of mind.

It may be instinctive to concentrate on what others have done to us, but taking a moment to reflect on where *we* may have been wrong, and acknowledging it, is fundamental to living a life of integrity.

Just for Today: Recognize that it is courageous to shift our focus from blaming others to taking responsibility for our actions.

| June 1 | Do Your Part |

Step 6 states that we "were entirely ready to have God remove all these defects of character." And Step 7 says that we "humbly asked Him to remove our shortcomings."

For years, I found those steps simple in theory, yet impossible to figure out in practice. I was looking in Step 7 for a magic fairy to tap me on the shoulder and BOOM all my defects would disappear. It never happened. One day, the simplicity of working these two steps became clear!

All you need to do in Step 6 is make a decision to take the action of Step 7, which is to become conscious of your defects as they arise, not act out on them, and work on practicing the opposite behavior. Then, your HP can work on gradually removing the defect.

For instance, when anger arises, pause and breathe through the feelings instead of reacting. If you are *really* in the "zone," practice compassion for the object of your anger.

Just for Today: Remember the words of the Chinese philosopher Lao Tzu, "Watch your thoughts; they become words. Watch your words; they become actions. Watch your actions; they become habit. Watch your habits; they become character. Watch your character; it becomes your destiny."

June 2   Tracking Sporadic Income

Those who receive a steady paycheck can easily create a spending plan. However, those who earn money on an unscheduled basis may find that creating a spending plan is daunting. Such people often protest that there is no way to keep a spending plan. But this is not an insurmountable obstacle. The ideal way to approach this issue is to "live in the next month." This means that the money you earn in the *current* month is spent in the *following* month, so you *always* know at the beginning of each month how much money is available to fund your categories. To make this work, you need enough savings to supply the first month's income. While many of us don't have that, we can create a category called "Buffer" and fund it monthly until we reach the goal of one month's income. Another suggestion is to average your last 12 months income. Use that number as your baseline monthly income number to fund your categories. Some months you may have more money to fund categories, which will make up for any shortfall in the months you have less.

Just for Today: Do you see that when we are willing to dive into solving a problem instead of using it as an excuse to stay stuck, we will find that the solution will come easier than we imagined?

June 3 — Live in Peace

In trying to live a life of peace, when we are wronged we are told on page 67 of the Big Book to show the "tolerance, pity, and patience that we would cheerfully grant a sick friend." But wouldn't this extend to harms perpetrated by anyone, anywhere? If not, wouldn't the Big Book say that it is OK to be enraged at the court system if you disagree with a verdict or the government if they don't behave as you would like? Instead, the Big Book tells us on page 66, "But with the alcoholic, whose hope is the maintenance and growth of a spiritual experience, this business s of resentment is infinitely grave. We found that it is fatal … If we were to live, we had to be free of anger."

Just for Today: Extend your tolerance, pity, and patience to harms done by others throughout the world, understanding that this does not mean you condone the acts.

June 4 — Visions Cost Money to Fulfill

In D.A., we are encouraged to have visions for our recovery life. This process can become confusing and frustrating because most visions, no matter how spiritually invested, involve some costs to fulfill. For instance, climbing Mt. Everest, swimming with dolphins, starting a business, meeting a soul mate, attending a spiritual retreat, most every vision requires at least a modest amount of capital to fund.

Having a vision is healthy. Bankrupting ourselves to achieve it prematurely is in opposition to the spirit of our program. For some of us, visions set obsession in motion. Newcomers to recovery may be especially vulnerable to living with the discomfort of waiting when their Higher Power seems to be guiding them to pursue a dream.

While money is the means to achieving our visions, it is only one piece of the puzzle. In recovery, we also have our commitment to balanced spending, saving, and living within our means as additional spiritual components.

Just for Today: Some of us have come to believe that the best recovery vision is simply taking the next right action and letting our Higher Power lead us to what is best for us instead of painfully trying to force an outcome when we cannot have what we want today.

June 5 — Enthusiasm

If we shove business, acclaim, and creativity into a single basket how will we ever find our true passion? Maybe we need to discover our creative potential by focusing on what makes our heart sing first… rather than on our pocketbook.

If, when we have a creative idea, our first thought is, "How can I make money at this?", we are more likely to move ahead without spending the time to develop our passion. And in the process of turning a new idea into a business prematurely, we may lose any enthusiasm we had and come to hate the idea as much as any day job.

Instead, we may first want to find our joy in doing the work without any thought of money or acclaim. We can then ask our Higher Power to give us clarity about the true purpose of the creative endeavor, to show us whether it is in our highest good to turn our process into a product.

Just for Today: If you find yourself considering passionless creating only for money, remember the words of Ralph Waldo Emerson, "Nothing great was ever achieved without enthusiasm."

June 6   Finding Balance

We are told that we must give back what we have so generously been given. We certainly don't want to water down the program or make excuses for why we can't do the basic requirements. However, we must also be cautious not to burn out by insisting we fulfill service requirements that may be impossible to achieve within our current lifestyle. We come into D.A. for relief from our pain. As we recover, we receive the gifts of this program and our life gets fuller. While we want to continue giving back, there has to be a balance between recovery work and living that new life with which we are now blessed. Recovery takes a lot of time and effort, and everyone, no matter what the circumstances, feels weighed down at first. That is the price of withdrawal from the disease of compulsive debting. However, once we are committed to a life in recovery, over the course of months or even years, we seek to find the right balance of program work with life commitments. If we feel we are burning out, we talk to our sponsors and support network to help us determine where we might take a step back.

Just for Today: Remember that program comes first, but we are also allowed to enjoy the fruits of our recovery as well.

June 7 — Persistence, Not Perfection

Some of us believe that the goal of recovery is to be defect-free, but, as the Big Book states on page 60: "No one among us has been able to maintain anything like perfect adherence to these principles. We are not saints. The point is that we are willing to grow along spiritual lines." Isn't it true that we have far more spiritual growth when life is rocky and we work through it without debting, compulsively spending, or hoarding than when all is going our way and we have the delusion that it will stay that way? When everything is going our way, we may become complacent, grasping to hold on to the status quo, forgetting this immutable law of nature: Nothing ever stays the same. Impermanence is the only sure thing. In order to continue to grow spiritually, there must be "something" to work on. Recovery is our willingness to persistently work on that ever-changing "something" every time it crops up. Defects spring up repeatedly requiring continual effort over time to lessen their effects on us. The goal may be to be free of our defects, but most of us must be satisfied with patient effort toward this goal.

Just for Today: We must remember that we are on a lifelong journey on the river of Improvement, not a short ride to the land of Perfection.

June 8 — Justifying Relapse

If we collapse in the face of challenges to our recovery and revert to throwing money at our problems or further depriving ourselves, we are not using the program as a practice to help us gain Faith and become restored to sanity. We need to recognize that recovery doesn't mean our problems disappear, nor should it. It means that we now live on a level playing field and are blessed with tools to deal with life on life's terms without acting out in our addiction.

When we slip or relapse, we don't eliminate the original problem. We simply create a layer of new problems on top of the one(s) we already had. When we experience the inevitable hangover after acting out with money, we may be left with self-loathing. Plus, we will now need to clean up newly created wreckage, which may include a fracture to relationships that may have been healed before we acted out.

Just for Today: Think about the repercussions of acting out with money when faced with problems, and turn to the D.A. tools instead of self-destructing.

June 9   Merging Money

In recovery, we learn how to manage our money. For those who are contemplating marriage or living together, the question of what to do about joint finances will come up. There is a strong societal push to join not only our lives, but our bank accounts.

However, in recovery we are cautious before merging our funds with another person. To begin with, we take our time to watch how the partner manages his or her money over time. If we see a pattern of unsecured debt continuing or increasing, we pause to consider how joining finances will affect our own recovery.

Managing money is a practical matter. It is not the measure of love between partners. There is no shame in keeping separate bank accounts and spending plans. It does not mean that the couple is not committed to the relationship.

Many couples successfully follow this formula. Joint bills can be handled in many ways, such as maintaining a checking account for this purpose or one partner reimbursing the other.

Just for Today: Remembering that money is a contentious issue in relationships, we do all we can to keep it simple.

June 10   Hobby or Business?

We hear a lot of talk about visions in D.A.. Some of us want to throw ourselves (and our money) into making the dream happen come what may, instead of taking the more measured D.A./BD.A. approach. This is often the case with a hobby that we believe could provide income. We may feel an urgency to go full throttle even if we do not have the money available, telling ourselves that it is an investment that will provide a return before we've done any research to support this claim. At this moment, the prudent course would be to slow down instead of speed up. PRGs can be invaluable in helping us find a way to monetize a hobby without debting or spending down our savings, and the BD.A. tools are a blueprint to sanely starting a business. As we take steps to convert a hobby into a business, we want to stay conscious of how we feel as we go down the path. If we find ourselves sinking more and more money with no return, or if our efforts make us miserable, resentful, and blocked instead of creatively energized … we may want to reconsider our decision.

Just for Today: Enjoyable hobbies are a precious commodity. The fact is, there are few things we do that make our heart sing, so when we find one, we may want to treat it with great care.

June 11 — Service at Meetings

Since we already attend meetings to enhance our recovery, why not use this opportunity to do service without impacting our schedule? Though there are committed service positions, such as literature or treasurer, there are plenty of other opportunities to serve during the meeting. Meeting leaders often have difficulty finding members who are willing to read, especially on phone meetings. We can all help out by having a copy of the format and readings available to us so we can participate. Beginners may not feel comfortable sharing at a meeting, but they can become involved by being timekeeper or reading. As we grow in recovery, we may want to offer to be the newcomer greeter or take phone numbers to distribute after the meeting. For those who meet the solvency requirement, leading a meeting, instead of sitting back and assuming someone else will step up, is service of the highest order, because without a leader, there is no meeting. Aside from helping others, doing service at meetings gives members a way to get to know us, enabling us to feel a sense of comfort and belonging more quickly.

Just for Today: Get a copy of the meeting format for your Home group and commit to doing service at the meeting on a regular basis.

June 12 — Layaway

The definition of layaway is placing a deposit on an item so the store holds it until the balance is paid in full. Is this a safe way to purchase for a compulsive debtor? In theory, this idea is equivalent to taking out a secured loan, which is an abstinent way to make a large purchase. However, we usually lay away a discretionary item, one which we could just as easily save for and then purchase outright. In addition, there may be fees associated with the layaway, such as a cancellation fee if you don't take the item, a store service fee, or a restocking fee if you make late payments or do not pay the balance by the due date. Sometimes, what we think we want so desperately becomes much less desirable over time … or if something else replaces it. When we commit to future purchasing, we are locked into a decision. And even with the best of intentions, circumstances can change. In order to protect ourselves, if we do enter into a layaway situation, we want to familiarize ourselves with the payment terms and potential loss we could incur should an unforeseen situation arise that keeps us from completing the purchase.

Just for Today: Before taking action, talk to your PRG team, sponsor, and network about whether it is a better decision to save for a purchase or enter into a layaway agreement.

June 13 — Communications Is Vital

As painful as it is to keep telling a creditor you cannot pay what you owe again and again, it is a great practice in humility and willingness to do so, both of which are two core components of living in recovery.

One strategy that may be helpful is agreeing with the collector that you want to pay the debt. The more you find common ground with someone, the more likely they will soften up. And even if they don't, you are doing your part to live in integrity.

Creditors and collections people are doing their job ... which may be in conflict with what you are able to do in recovery. But if you cannot give someone what they want, running away and not dealing with it only inflames the situation.

Just for Today: Are you willing to face life's challenges?

June 14 — Fellowship and Faith

D.A. promises that if we work our program, "Isolation will give way to fellowship; faith will replace fear." We are blessed to have a fellowship full of others just like us when it comes to money. Meetings abound in person, online, and on the phone. People are generous in giving out their contact information so we can connect in sponsorship, PRGs, and outreach. All we have to do is show up, which can be the hardest part. Perhaps that is the only positive aspect of our addiction, that we eventually hit a bottom that forces us to reach out for help.

As for faith replacing fear, that is a by-product of our involvement with this program. We begin by having faith that the miracles that have happened to others can happen to us, which we hear about in meetings and outreach calls. Eventually, our faith turns to belief when we have the experience ourselves. We keep the fellowship alive by sharing that experience with others at meetings and in outreach calls, reminding ourselves that the key to getting and staying sober with money is service to others.

Just for Today: Think about this -- if we don't actively participate in the fellowship, how will the program survive?

June 15 — Acceptance Is the Key

When we live in today and accept what we cannot change, we agree that we will not purchase items we cannot afford. But agreeing and accepting is not necessarily the same thing.

We can agree, yet act out with rage, kicking and screaming about not getting what we want. We can try to justify the spending by telling ourselves that it's our money and we are not debting ... though such willfulness can be the first step toward relapse.

Or we can choose to live in the solution, which is to accept that our disease may kick up in the form of obsession and desire, but our recovery can keep us from acting on it or making it worse for ourselves. We can ask for help to keep from making the purchase and be willing to sit in the discomfort until it passes, knowing that we are making a sane and sober decision.

If we remember that acceptance is the key to all our difficulties for today, then we can relax peacefully into the present and enjoy what is in front of us, rather than focusing resentfully on what we don't yet possess.

Just for today: Try to remember that eventually, we can purchase what we want if we still want it when the funds are available.

June 16   Progress, Not Perfection

In recovery, we learn not to take what isn't ours, even if we can convince ourselves that it doesn't hurt anyone. From pirated software to movies to music to books, we gradually learn to pay for what we use. Some people say, "Corporations don't mind cheating us, and they overcharge for so many items, so why not just take what you can." But can we live by that philosophy and stay sober?

Our morality doesn't depend on what others do, just as our sobriety doesn't. We need to stay physically and emotionally sober; to do what is right within our own heart that brings us peace. A peaceful heart is a grateful heart and they say that a grateful heart doesn't binge.

Just for Today: If you think of taking something that isn't rightfully yours without paying for it, think about whether it will erode your abstinence. If you can't afford it, think about the spiritual lesson in delayed gratification and ask yourself if the price is worth the cost?

June 17 — Preference and Desire

Becoming "drunk with desire" is dangerous for those in recovery because it pumps adrenaline into the system of compulsive debtors and spenders, whose recovery depends upon seeking a peaceful existence. Preference doesn't have grasping associated with it, and allows for not getting what we want without emotional upheaval. When we do not have the funds to purchase what we yearn for, yet let desire drive us, we are in opposition to our Higher Power's will for us, which is to live within our means. But addicts caught in the clutches of desire can be excellent at justifying what they want. Desire can make us feel out of control and desperate. Desperation is anathema to recovery. When we feel that pressing, overwhelming urge to purchase an item we cannot afford, we can wait as a gesture of solidarity with our recovery and our Higher Power. Sometimes just waiting a day is enough, but it could be a week, a month, or even longer, until the raging inferno dies down. This waiting may be new behavior and very uncomfortable. But as we learn in recovery, everything passes, and if we don't give in to the obsession, our disease eventually backs off and desire becomes preference, or may disappear entirely.

Just for Today: Are you willing to choose preference over desire?

June 18 — Sometimes...

Sometimes, even with the best of intentions, life throws us a curveball and we must veer from our ideal path. The Big Book states on page 60 that "no one among us has been able to maintain anything like perfect adherence to these principles."

Such is the case when we are committed to living within our means, but health or other urgent concerns force us to dip into our savings. In these cases, we can remind ourselves that we are not debting, even though we may suffer concern about the future if there are no savings left.

While we take the next right action to solve the problem, we are open to other ways to accomplish the goal. Before taking action, we will want to seek counsel from our Higher Power, a PRG team, sponsor, and/or network.

For many of us, our time in recovery is the first we have ever accumulated savings, and we may want to do everything in our power to keep it intact. We also keep a separate Contingency fund for emergencies, which may contain $1,000 or more. However, acceptance may mean that we need more than what we have saved in Contingency to address the situation.

Just for Today: While we do not frivolously spend down our savings, that money is ours to use for a serious, unexpected, or emergency situation.

June 19   Facing Fear of Death

Most of us have a fear of death. We avoid thinking about such unpleasant matters, but doing so can enhance our recovery and actually reduce our fear around it. Life is filled with opportunities to practice. For instance, when we enter recovery and decide not to incur new unsecured debt, isn't that a kind of death? It is the end of an old way of life, and it can be terrifying to leave behind the familiar and "safe," even if that is the way to destruction. When we first cut up our credit cards, we are terrified that a catastrophe will befall us that we cannot fund. But most of us discover that this catastrophe never happens and, instead, we have actually accumulated savings to address an emergency! By following the D.A. admonition of living "one day at a time," it is far easier to deal with our fears, even the fear of death and certainly the fear of needing credit for a crisis. If we stick to our spending plan, when fear arises, we can look squarely at it and see if it is imagined or appropriate. Embracing new perceptions and practices gives us the ability to live with our discomfort and suffer less around it.

Just for Today: Don't run from your fears. Stop for a moment and look squarely at them. Most likely, you will find they are just future imaginings having no basis in today's reality.

June 20   Patience as a Spiritual Practice

Practicing patience is a powerful spiritual tool. It may be easier to practice while waiting than when dealing with difficult people. But the more we practice patience during delays, the easier it may become to exhibit patience with others. When interacting with others, we often cannot catch our impatience in time because of the pace and escalation intertwined with communication. But when we have to wait or are delayed (for instance, at the doctor's office, on the highway, at the airport), we have time and space to become acutely aware of what impatience feels like. We see that we have choices. We can fume, tense up, and possibly take it out on others. Or we can acknowledge the feelings without acting out on them, and instead close our eyes, calm our breathing, pray for acceptance, and keep our delay in perspective.

Just for Today: The next time you are stuck in traffic or your travel is otherwise stalled, use the opportunity to practice gratitude, acceptance, and peace.

June 21   The Value of Silence

Publilius Syrus, the Roman writer said, "I have often regretted my speech, never my silence." When I was in my 20's, I was socially awkward, self-conscious, and talked way too much. A dear friend taught me an invaluable lesson. She was (and still is) a delightful and charming woman who is a sought-after guest. The key to her success and comfort in social situations is her ability to listen to others.

When we focus on others, asking them questions and following up, showing an interest in their lives, people feel validated and heard. Plus, our anxiety dissipates because we are focusing on the other person, rather than on what they think of us.

Giving service is key to keeping what we have. Giving service is not only sharing our own recovery, but reaching out to help the still suffering compulsive debtor. Listening well without giving advice is at the heart of Step 12.

We learn how to work our program by listening to others who have what we want at meetings, on outreach calls, with sponsors, and in our PRGs. We learn to listen to our Higher Power by meditation.

Just for Today: Is there any more powerful reason to cultivate the ability to listen well than enhancing the quality of our recovery?

June 22 — Hearing or Listening?

Active listening requires more than just hearing what others have to say. An intimate dialog is comprised of validating and going deeper into what the speaker is saying by asking follow-up questions.

This is a good practice to put into effect when we make our D.A. outreach calls. Often, we need to vent about our own issue, but when we are done, we might ask how the other person is doing, not as an obligatory gesture, but with genuine interest. Too often, people give lip service to this concept, boomeranging back to themselves without even a comment. It is often obvious that they are not really interested in what the other person has to say.

Active listening is about focusing your attention on the speaker, rather than being absorbed in what you want to say next; not trying to one-up or compete; not giving advice or proving that you know more.

While we do listen to others, it is also imperative that we speak our truth in order to recover. We don't confuse listening with co-dependent silence.

Just for Today: It is OK to be cautious with whom we share our issues, taking care to do so with those who also practice active listening to ensure we get our own needs met.

June 23   What Does Fame Feel Like?

After nearly five decades of (unsuccessfully) pursuing fame, I finally understand that fame is not a feeling. It is the desire for fame, watching others who are famous when you, yourself, yearn for it, that generates the *idea* of that feeling. Fame is just a state of being that is bestowed and removed in a heartbeat by others over whom we have no control. Many people describe that when they get accolades or acclaim, it feels nice for a brief moment, and then they go about their day.

For some of us, when we don't experience that ultimate "ahhhhh," we lose the passion for what we are doing. Too often, we didn't really have a passion for the work itself, but a desire for a certain reaction from others that we thought would fulfill us. People who feel passion for their work regardless of the outcome are the ones who describe that feeling of deep and profound joy. The feeling we keep reaching for is like grasping at water; impossible to hold. But when we get lost in the act of creation, doing what we love, the feeling we yearn for spreads throughout our body. It is a joy, meaning, and sense of accomplishment that doesn't occur when others reflect back to us, but when we are in the experience.

Just for Today: Can you find joy in the doing instead of seeking it only in the result?

June 24 — Just Say No

When we are in the throes of our addiction, it may seem as if we are slaves to the stuff we buy. In recovery, we learn that we have choices when it comes to our spending no matter how loudly an obsession calls to us.

We develop strength of character when we see we are not powerless against every whim that comes along. We learn to see our addiction for the coward that it really is, instead of the bully it pretends to be.

Each time we say no to spending compulsively or giving in when we cannot afford a purchase, we learn that the pain of saying no is not bottomless.

By going to meetings, working the steps and the tools, and creating a network with sponsors, PRG teams, and outreach, we cloak ourselves in the grace and protection of our Higher Power, and experience the relief that comes when we live within our means.

Just for Today: Allow yourself to feel the warm and loving embrace of your Higher Power.

June 25 — Overwhelm

We can get overwhelmed by all we need to do to stay sober. Unlike some addictions, we can't just say no. All 12 step programs involve sponsoring, meetings, working the steps, and outreach. But in D.A., we have a whole other set of tasks we need to do, which involve skills that many of us find challenging.

In recovery, many of us write down our spending, develop and live by a spending plan, attend and give PRGs, and reconcile our spending plan with our bank accounts. Some of us also commit our money before we spend it and do daily step reading and writing. In addition, some of us have to deal with creditors and gather information on our debts. That may seem like a tall order for a newcomer.

We don't walk in and do every single thing at once. This is a gradual learning process, beginning with writing down what we spend. Step 1 is the admission of powerlessness over our drug. In D.A., we also begin our journey by removing vagueness around our spending.

Just for Today: Even as we progress in recovery, we may find ourselves feeling overwhelmed periodically. That is when we remember to just do first things first ... one thing at a time.

June 26   There Is Enough

D.A. Promises that if we work the program, "we will recognize that there is enough; our resources will be generous and we will share them with others and with D.A.." Grasping and craving are in opposition to this promise. Recovery first helps us see these defects in ourselves and then gives us the tools to be relieved of them. For instance, when we give service, we share our recovery. We don't keep information to ourselves that could be of benefit to another addict. When we believe that we have enough just for today, we feel more peaceful. We see that jealousy of what others have moves us away from the Spirit. While we may still feel fearful under certain financial circumstances, we turn to our Higher Power and our network for help. Our generous resources may not manifest as money, but as time, experience, and selfless giving to others. Once we have experienced getting through a crisis without debting, we can then generously share our experience, strength, and hope with others in D.A., and use the experience as an anchor to remind ourselves of the truth when future fear causes us to experience grasping and craving once again.

Just for Today: We remember that what is ours will come to us and there is plenty of room in this universe for each person's unique success and achievements.

June 27 — The Future

When we find ourselves fearing future financial catastrophe, we can bring ourselves back to this present moment and become aware of what is happening right now. Focusing on the past, which no longer exists, and the future, which hasn't happened yet, is a huge waste of our time on earth, and a distraction from the work we could be doing today to achieve our goals.

All we have is each passing moment. Being as present as we can today is the best use of our time. We build our future by our present actions. So if we live consciously in the present, we can let go of what will happen in the future.

Just for Today: When you find yourself in fear about the future, instead focus on what you can do today to create the life you want.

June 28 — Our Assets

How quickly and severely I judge myself for every misstep. I always looked at the glass as half empty. Today, I am working toward seeing it as half full. When we do our daily 10th step inventory, it's easy to be hard on ourselves by focusing on what we did "wrong." While it is vital that we take responsibility for our inartful actions, we also want to ask ourselves how we were kind and loving and what we did well.

Addicts can live in the extreme; all good or all bad. Recovery teaches us a middle way even with those who harm us. We learn that we need to let go of our resentments, to take responsibility when we are at fault, and to find compassion in our hearts when others wrong us. It's not always easy, but it's always in our best interest to do so. A heart filled with hate is not healthy.

Therefore, we seek to remind ourselves of our positive efforts when we review our day, even on the most challenging of them. We must learn to appreciate the good in ourselves as well as make the effort to remove our defects. A daily inventory that includes assets as well as deficits helps us to learn balance.

Just for Today: Recovery teaches us to value ourselves innately and not in comparison with others.

June 29 — Acceptance and Gratitude

Acceptance helps us get through hard times and releases us from the past's stranglehold. Acceptance doesn't mean that we just sit in a bad situation or feelings. Acceptance means that we are not fighting our current reality. Once we accept what is happening, we can come to see what we can change and take the next right action to do so.

Gratitude is a vital aid to acceptance. They say a grateful heart doesn't binge or debt. A grateful heart doesn't sink into resentment and wallow in regret, self-pity, and longing. We can write gratitudes every single day. No matter how difficult our current life situation, there is always something for which we can be grateful.

Just for Today: The Serenity Prayer can be a soothing companion during difficult times.

June 30 — Determined Effort

The principle behind Step 6 is willingness. Without willingness, there is no recovery. Acting on these principles and, indeed, on the steps of this program takes a determined effort of willingness.

Addicts do not like discomfort and there is inevitable pain in learning a new way of being in the world and within yourself. When you feel yourself bristle at the suggestions of your PRG team or sponsor, instead of hardening your heart to the idea, soften to their suggestions, and open to the possibility of becoming willing to at least try the approach suggested.

Just for Today: When you find people in program who have what you want, ask how they achieved it ... and become willing to do what they did.

July 1 — Removing Our Shortcomings

Step 7 states that we "humbly asked Him to remove our shortcomings." There is nothing in these steps that says I will not feel my feelings, but that doesn't mean I need to destroy everyone and everything in sight when I do feel destructive emotions.

As it says in the Big Book on page 60, "We are not saints. The point is that we are willing to grow along spiritual lines. The principles we have set down are guides to progress. We claim spiritual progress rather than spiritual perfection." Once we are angry, it may feel like it is too late to stop that freight train from barreling over the person who has incited our wrath.

Gradually, we *can* change on the inside. But it starts on the outside, by changing our behavior. If we do our part, our Higher Power can heal us on a deeper level. The point is that with practice, we can partner with our Higher Power to reduce and ultimately remove our defects of character – first the action, and then the emotion around it.

Just for Today: With practice, we can learn what triggers us, and learn to move away, instead of toward, the defect.

July 2 — Slaves to Our Defects

Nowhere in the Big Book does it say that our defects will be removed permanently and instantly, never to return. When we feel angry and turn that into love we feel much better about ourselves than when we act out on the emotion and cause harm and pain to those around us.

We aren't talking about sublimating anger, but transforming it, which can only come with practice. Even if we are not free from emotions such as anger, by practicing, we come to know from experience, that we *do* have a choice. We are no longer a slave to our defects as long as we continue to be willing to grow along spiritual lines and practice the opposite of our defects when they arise. We may not always succeed, but sometimes we will, and isn't that improvement in our behavior what practice is about?

Just for Today: Embrace each opportunity to practice the opposite of your defects.

July 3 — Self-Care

While it is important for us to give back what we have received, some of us burn out overdoing service, and for those people an important part of recovery is learning how to set boundaries. However, there are many ways in which we can give back generously without burning ourselves out. For instance, leading a meeting or being time-keeper are invaluable ways to give back at a time when you are already involved in a D.A. activity. When you make a phone call, ask the person on the other end of the phone how they are doing. Both listening and revealing your truth, when you are suffering, are crucial to success in D.A. and important ways to give back. We keep our recovery by giving generously of ourselves *as we are able* so that we can help others. Remembering that we must respect our own boundaries, even in 12th Step work, is another way we help others learn good self-care, which is essential to our recovery.

Just for Today: Don't forget that if we don't take care of ourselves, we are much more likely to relapse in our addiction.

July 4 — Freedom

Page 83 of the Big Book promises us that "we are going to know a new freedom and a new happiness." The 4th of July is the day to celebrate freedom, and happiness comes along for the ride. Happiness is a dangerous word when the perceived lack of it is used as an excuse to act out in our addiction. This "new happiness" is not a euphoric state dependent on all our wishes coming true. Happiness is our ability to be OK no matter what happens; it is not about getting our way, which, in retrospect, never made us all that happy. Ironically, it is through the discipline of living by a spending plan and within our means that we truly become free. When we spent our lives endlessly trying to satisfy craving after craving, we were shackled with suffering. In D.A. we have the opportunity to practice delayed gratification, which teaches us to release craving. Living by a spending plan enables us to accrue money in categories, which gives us the freedom to select what spending is most important to us. How liberating it is to be able to handle our increasing resources in a healthy manner without resorting to our old compulsive ways.

Just for Today: Be grateful that you don't have to live by the seat of your pants, enslaved to craving, any longer. We are free because we plan. What an irony for an addict.

July 5 — We are Not Our Debts

If we are to recover, we cannot allow ourselves to be defined by our debts, to permit creditors, collection agents, or our own self-judgment to diminish ourselves. We came into program to learn a new way to coexist with money that is not destructive.

The issue of debt is an incredibly painful one, but must be brought into the light of clarity along with a realistic spending plan and ongoing reconciliation of our numbers in order to recover from this disease.

The reality of communicating with creditors in honesty and humility is far less frightening than the imagined terror we're avoiding by ignoring the phone calls and letters. Facing our fears often puts everything in perspective. As D.A. Promise #10 states: "We will no longer fear the truth; we will move from hiding in denial to living in reality."

Just for Today: There is nothing about our financial situation, no matter how dire, that is worse than the torture we impose on ourselves when we refuse to face it.

July 6 — Do I Deserve That?

What constitutes a luxury? I was surprised that I came up against this issue the other day when I was buying clothes. I've longed for nightgowns and pajamas, yet felt they were frivolous luxuries, so generally sleep in sweatpants and whatever shirt is handy. Having a limited amount of money for clothing, I want to make the right spending decision, which seems to be to only buy clothes used in the world, not items that I will only wear to bed.

This may seem silly to normal people who have always worn nighttime clothing. But don't we each have something in our recovery that may seem frivolous or too much, even if it is not expensive?

The point is that by not living in disease with money, splurging and debting, or, alternatively, hoarding and depriving, we are able to incorporate items that once seemed out of reach or too luxurious for us to deserve. We are now able, in recovery, to begin to reach for what we desire in a sane and sober manner.

Just for Today: Without whipping yourself into a frenzy of desire, see if there is a luxury, no matter how small, you can afford in your spending plan.

July 7   Talking to Kids About Money

In many families, a personal discussion about money is taboo. Compulsive debtors and spenders may feel too ashamed about their out-of-control spending and debting to talk about it. But even so-called normal families have issues around being open on this subject. Without open communication, children may come to believe that managing money is a mysterious skill. But the fact is that most of us deal with money nearly every day. With proper communication, children learn that money is not mystical tool like a magic wand, but a practical implement like a key.

Some compulsive debtors and spenders live a lie with their children by purchasing anything their hearts desire even when the adults can't afford it, leading their children to believe that money does, indeed, grow on trees. By talking honestly and humbly about our financial situation with our children, we can do our part to help them understand limitations and boundaries when they are young. And if we don't talk to our children about money in a personal way, how on earth are they expected to learn how to manage it when they grow up?

Just for Today: Think about what a difference it would make if an entire generation of young people learned from the start how to live within their means.

July 8 — Stand Strong

We have a sacred responsibility as PRG team members to speak our truth. It is a tough love road and not for the faint of heart. A PRG shows us the raw, stark truth about where we want to spend our money. If a PRG team member sees that we are not acting in our own self-interest, it is imperative that the truth be spoken. While the money belongs to us, we know that our best intentions are often clouded by addict thinking. Our immediate reaction when told that a choice we want to make is not sober may be to fire our team and find another who will tell us what we want to hear. But is that really the wisest course? It may be better to release our tight grasp on getting our way and allow ourselves to consider the guidance of our team. They are not there to thwart our efforts, but to guide us to sober use of our money. We may fight to get our way and become increasingly insistent in our efforts to convince our team that we are right. When we find ourselves reacting angrily and emotionally at our PRG team's suggestions, that may be the very moment that we should pause instead of proceeding. If our behavior around our financial choices is not sober, perhaps we need to take a closer look at the object of our friction.

Just for Today: The best PRG may be the one that causes you discomfort.

July 9 — Fearing the Truth

D.A. promises that if we work the program, "we will no longer fear the truth; we will move from hiding in denial to living in reality."

In D.A., our recovery is dependent on moving from hiding in denial to living in reality. For instance, in AA, we have to put the booze down so that I can move into reality. But in D.A., if we don't open our mail, we are hiding in denial. If we don't face our creditors, we are hiding in denial. If we don't have and live by a spending plan, we are hiding in denial.

Many of us have had to face terrible truths in our financial lives. And those who are truly working the program face these truths with equanimity. Everyone gets frightened, but in recovery, we have tools to lessen, and even remove, the fear.

Some say that when the pain we are trying to avoid by using our drug becomes greater than the pain we experience by using, we will stop. So, too, when the pain avoidance and murkiness create becomes worse than just facing the truth, we will be willing to step into the light.

Just for Today: Do you believe that the truth will set you free?

July 10   The Spending Plan's Potential

The spending plan is an incredible tool to bring clarity into our lives and create order out of financial chaos. But we must fully embrace all that the spending plan has to offer if we want to reap the rewards. We can create categories for our wants and needs. Some people separate their spending more broadly and some with more detail. But having categories is how we keep track of where our money goes. We accrue in categories to save for what we want and need. Doing so removes the frenzy to find the funds when bills are due. We can assign every dollar we earn to a category. Doing so ensures our money has a purpose and prevents us from thinking funds are available when they truly aren't. We can talk our decision through with our sponsor or PRG team members before shifting money between categories. Doing so will keep us from leaving ourselves short if we intend to take money from a category that must stay funded. We can set up a PRG when we are struggling to make ends meet. Doing so will help us get out of the pain that vagueness around money can cause. Having a PRG every few months keeps us in reality and helps us work through financial challenges.

Just for Today: Are you using your spending plan to its fullest potential?

July 11 — Anger and Sadness

For many addicts, anger may actually mask sadness. For some, anger makes them feel more in control. Sadness can feel like a blanket that is smothering us. But anger is a weapon that we brandish and use to hurt others. When we put the weapon down, we can then feel the blanket of sadness pressing on us and work lovingly to remove it by dealing with the underlying issues.

In addition, for many of us, adrenaline is core to our addiction. We can't use our drug anymore to get high. Anger provides a great adrenaline rush, so instead of feeling sad, we get angry. In recovery, we learn how to feel the unpleasant feelings, the ones we're not used to feeling; the ones that make us want to crawl out of our skin; the ones that are at our core.

But this is not easy for most addicts, who avoid any level of discomfort. So we remind ourselves that emotional pain will not kill us, that it will pass, and that the payoff is a more peaceful life.

Just for Today: We remember that when we let ourselves feel our sadness instead of using anger to mask it, the feelings eventually lift without leaving a string of people to whom we need to make amends after the storm has passed.

July 12   A New Way of Thinking

Albert Einstein said, "No problem can be solved from the same level of consciousness that created it." How true this is for compulsive debtors. We can't possibly recover from this hopeless state of mind and body by using the same way of thinking we used in the past.

D.A. teaches us how to think differently. Where we once made all our financial decisions on our own, we now confer with others before making major decisions around our money. We no longer shoot from the hip in our spending, but live by a spending plan, in which we divide our money into categories. We plan out our spending so that we accrue money we will need for quarterly or annual bills, instead of scrambling at the last minute to figure out how to pay them. We fund our visions over time because we no longer act on impulse. We also learn how to live more harmoniously with others. We do this by changing our consciousness around our own actions. We learn how to think before we speak, being mindful that we will have to make amends if we cause harm by speech or action.

Just for Today: We are grateful that there is a proven path to show us how to shift our consciousness so we can solve our compulsive debting and spending problem one day at a time.

July 13 — Partner Challenges

There can be intense challenges facing recovering debtors and spenders who have partners. If both partners share the same addiction and only one partner gets into recovery, this can cause additional stress. If one partner does not share the addiction, there may be lingering trust issues long after the afflicted partner walks the path of recovery.

Either way, we must find a way to manage our financial lives despite these issues. For those with partners who still suffer with the addiction, it may be best to separate the income and spending. If that is not feasible, the recovering partner might take charge of the spending plan and paying the bills. In cases where the non-addicted partner has previously controlled the money, the recovering member may want to take responsibility for certain categories and bills.

We can reach out to our Higher Power and to others for experience, strength, and hope to figure out how to navigate this long and winding road. Eventually, those who stay in recovery find a way that works within their partnership. There is always a way. But, as with so much in recovery, it may take some time to discover it.

Just for Today: Do not give up hope if it seems that maintaining your solvency is out of your hands.

July 14   Slow and Steady Practice

We may delude ourselves into thinking that by doing what we need to do to get and stay sober with money that all our money problems will mysteriously disappear. Once we realize this isn't true, we may become demoralized. Instead, let us consider our program and the actions we take to stay solvent as a way to practice and improve our spiritual condition.

Working Steps 6 & 7 is seeing our defects rise up and practicing the opposite quality *over and over* which gives our Higher Power the opportunity to remove the deeper emotions. The hold that some of our defects have on us may never disappear entirely, but with persistent practice, we can be sure that we will be spiritually improved.

Just for Today: Our spiritual growth is a direct result of consistent practice ... not in thinking we are failures if we don't achieve perfection as a result.

July 15   Reflection

Prayer is asking for direction from a Higher Power. Meditation is listening for answers. Reflection is the study of ways to turn the answers we get from meditation into action.

Too many times, the "brainstorm" in the quiet of meditation turns out to be nothing more than self-will run riot. It is by learning new skills in D.A., such as waiting 24 hours, having a PRG, seeking ESH from others, or writing about the issue that we begin to understand the value of reflection.

Sometimes, what we think of as a vision is really just a way for our disease to act out. Waiting is a spiritual process that forces reflection when it is coupled with open discussion with others in recovery. Some of us also suffer with an affliction called "instant gratification" that is closely connected with compulsive spending, one symptom of which is a hole burned in our pockets when we have accumulated money. Prayer, meditation, and reflection together lead to recovery helping us discern our will from our Higher Power's. Unless we pass the answers we receive through the filter of our program, by reflection, we cannot get to the truth.

Just for Today: Waiting is the simplest form of reflection.

July 16   Relationship Anonymity

Anonymity is the spiritual foundation of our program. We do not have to tell anyone about our addiction or recovery. That's what makes us feel safe. But, what do we do when we enter into a new relationship? Concerns about when it is appropriate to share our experience with someone else are bound to come up when we are getting to know another person.

Eventually, money will creep into the conversation. We can share our recovery attitude without sharing information about our past addiction if we don't want to; just as we may choose to not reveal other personal or health information to someone we are just getting to know.

If we do not have the funds for an activity or need to select a restaurant that will comfortably fit into our spending plan, we can simply say so. This is an opportunity to practice humility and acceptance. While it may be uncomfortable to admit our limitations when we used to be the big spender, keeping it simple may be the best option so that the moment passes quickly.

Just for Today: At the point that we feel it is appropriate to share our past addiction with another person, we can do so without feeling ashamed. We are now in recovery and our actions speak loudly regarding our commitment to sobriety with money.

July 17 — Action Plan

Recovery from compulsive debting and spending requires a lot of action on our part. We don't have the luxury of being able to refrain from using our drug (money); instead we must actively work to repair our relationship with it.

While we don't incur new unsecured debt or spend recklessly any longer, we must also take action to repair any financial damage we have caused in the past as well as to improve our financial situation in the present. We must also take the action of keeping our numbers to ensure clarity with our finances. Creating a spending plan follows soon after. Our sponsor, PRG team, and network can help us devise a plan to address all these issues one at a time.

Debt repayment and dealing with creditors can seem overwhelming. That is why we need a plan to do so. In the past, we flew by the seat of our pants. In recovery, we learn how to sort out what needs to be done and get the help we need to take the next right action.

Just for Today: Remember that you don't have to do this alone.

July 18 — A Work in Progress

Our spending plan isn't just there for show. It takes months to refine a spending so that it works within our lifestyle. Even then, we consider our spending plan a work in progress. Life changes, so our spending plan must be flexible. But still, the bones of the plan remain the same. For instance, we may need to add a new category if our life circumstance changes, such as if we purchase a home. We may need to eliminate a category, such as after we fully fund a special purchase. And we may need to shift priorities to increase the amount we accrue in a category, such as if we need more money for groceries. But overall, we no longer base our spending decisions on the amount available in our bank account. Instead, we look at our spending plan and base our spending on our categories. When our spending plan is properly configured, we see that all our money accounted for in a variety of categories, including Contingency, Savings, Prudent Reserve, and Charity, if possible.

Just for Today: When it looks as if a need or want can't be funded, we don't throw in the towel and turn away from our spending plan. That is the moment to schedule a PRG, where miracles around money are known to happen, and we experience gratitude for our sobriety and the flexibility of our spending plan.

July 19   Taking Care of Business

In recovery, we no longer ignore financial issues. Instead, we fix our problems. We can do this because we keep a spending plan and reconcile it with our bank account and cash. Today, we know if a merchant has overcharged us or the bank has made an error, and we address the problem instead of avoiding it. Another way we take care of business is returning items that are broken or don't fit. In our addiction, some of us would buy and compulsively return items. But for others of us, we just let them sit or threw them out. Today, we return items appropriately.

It's often challenging for newcomers to learn how to keep their spending plan reconciled with their bank account. And many of us spend frustrating hours unraveling issues when we first practice this process. The best way to learn how to manage all these functions is to stay on top of the situation. This may mean updating our spending plan daily and reconciling weekly or more until we have a handle on it. It also means that if we notice a bank error, we address it right away. And it means that we don't buy something intending to return it, but if that becomes necessary, we follow through.

Just for Today: Know that getting clear with your finances is possible if you are willing to deal with it.

July 20 — Accumulated Funds

If we are saving for an item, we accrue money monthly to pay for it. But what about money accumulated in fixed categories or those that are "use it or lose it?" Examples of fixed categories are mortgage, debt repayment, or electric bill. Examples of "Use it or lose it" categories are haircut and gas. I may have $50 saved monthly for a haircut, but if I only spent $40 on my haircut, the extra $10 will not be used toward another haircut. Or I allocate $100/month for gas, but only spent $80 this month, leaving $20.

In D.A., we try to properly fund our categories, but sometimes, these things happen. We do this so that there isn't just a "pile of money" lying around calling to us to be spent.

We may want to be patient and let the money sit in its category for a few months to see if these circumstances continue or we can work with our sponsor or PRG team to re-allocate the money.

We may see the extra money as a windfall, but if we get willing to seek guidance around shifting monthly amounts before taking the money for a joy ride, we may be reminded that we have categories that need additional funding.

Just for Today: We can be willing to sit with the discomfort of having extra money in a category for a short time without spending it.

July 21   Saving for What We Want

The concept of saving for what we want may be alien to us. In the past, we would scratch that itch immediately by using a credit card, or spending money that needed to be allocated for some other purpose, like food or rent.

In recovery, we don't have to despair if we want a bicycle or washing machine or big screen TV but don't have enough cash right now. We can add a category to our spending plan for this item and assign a dollar amount each month to accrue until we have enough to purchase it.

Stories abound in D.A. of people saving for months or years to acquire what they want. Though it may seem an eternity to save for two years to buy a top-of-the-line blender, as one D.A. member did, her joy of buying it abstinently made the purchase even sweeter and the memory of waiting evaporate.

Just for Today: Begin saving for something you want, even if you just put $1 toward it monthly.

July 22 — Shifting My Thinking

This pre-recovery thinking that money is magic still haunts us at times. But today, we are aware that it is a myth, and allowing ourselves to wallow in self-pity or feelings of deprivation is just going to lead us back to debting. Far better for us to turn our thoughts to gratitude for all we have and learn to be satisfied with our life today than waste our life wishing for tomorrow or worse, wishing for a reality that isn't.

It's hard for us to wait and accumulate for big purchases. But I remember saving up for a passport. I just allocated a small amount each month and let go of it. I stopped obsessing about it, even forgot about it. And a year later, I had a passport! A year after that, I went to Europe abstinently. Now THAT is a miracle.

God: Help us to remember to be grateful for what we have when we are faced with not being able to purchase what we want when we want it.

July 23 — Financial Choices

When I think about people who have a lot of money (which to me is pretty much any amount more than I have), what strikes me is that those people don't have to give a second thought to things that I have to give quite a lot of thought about.

For instance, if I choose to buy a book, I may not be able to go to a movie. Or I may have to wait until next month to buy either one. Or I may wonder if I can make my shampoo last until the next month because I'm short on personal care money. Some people can buy a book, go to a movie, buy shampoo, go out to dinner, buy a Ferrari, invest in a Picasso, and take a world cruise with cash and not think twice about it.

On the other hand, there are people who need to choose between food and medicine. So if our struggle is between a book and a movie or even making shampoo last a bit longer, are we really suffering compared to someone else? In fact, do we really need to suffer at all or is it just our attitude about the situation that causes us pain?

Just for Today: Is comparing our financial lot with others just a way to encourage resentment?

July 24 — Self-Worth

Recovery from compulsive debting and spending leads us to a renewed sense of self-worth. D.A. promises that "we will realize that we are enough; we will value ourselves and our contributions." Before recovery, our value was tied to our credit line and how others saw us. In recovery, we become humble and learn to live within our means. We accept that while our financial resources are *not* infinite, our ability to contribute to society *is*. We may still feel some residual self-judgment if we no longer have the fancy accoutrements we once had. And it is true that there *are* people who *will* judge us based on what we own, what we wear, and where we live. But spiritual growth and healing occurs when we shift our focus from how the world sees us to what we can do to better it on a personal level. There can be growing pains as we do this and it is not always a smooth road. But when the veils of delusion are finally lifted, the jewel of who we really are is revealed and we feel a sense of self-worth far greater than any falsely bestowed on us by our transient belongings and the opinion of others.

Just for Today: Let your value be measured by who you are and what you do, not by what you own and how much you spend.

July 25 — Category Detail

It's not just money for our needs that have to be allocated, but for our wants as well. We each need a different level of detail in our spending plan to maintain our recovery. It takes rigorous self-honesty to know the level of detail you require.

For instance, one person may need a separate category for Grocery and House Supplies and someone else may just allocate to a single category, with the understanding that anything from the supermarket, be it meat or paper towels, comes out of that category. I may need to have a category for shoes and another for clothing, and you may not need to separate them at all.

Whether your category boundaries are detailed or broad, having them is integral to recovery from compulsive debting and spending. If we take creating, maintaining, and living within our spending plan seriously, instead of just giving it lip service, we are guaranteed to stay debt-free, one day at a time.

Just for Today: Do your categories contain the right level of detail for you?

July 26   Passing Moments

We cannot hold on to moments. Each passes. So, for instance, two days ago, I took myself to a movie. It was a fabulous treat for me. I was alone in the theater seeing a great action movie, sitting in exactly the seat I wanted. Oh, how blissful it truly was for me. It was a simple pleasure and I wasn't gripped by painful desire, yet the experience was sheer delight.

Now, two days later where is that feeling? There is no way to hold on to time. And not all moments can be blissful. Sure, I would LOVE to recreate that experience. I am an addict and prefer peak experiences. But, for one thing, I don't have money left for movies this month. And for another, too much of a good thing loses its effect on me.

So, today, I sit here writing this passage, not feeling at all well. I can remember that experience in the movie theater (vaguely), but cannot be in it once it is over. That is the nature of life.

Just for Today: Let me work on acceptance that everything passes, good and bad.

July 27 — How to Apologize

In recovery, we learn that it is not enough to say we are sorry. It is also important to admit that we were wrong. There is a big difference in saying, "I am sorry that you felt hurt by what I said" and "I was wrong to say that." It may seem subtle, but Step Nine is about making amends for the wrongs we have done to others, without blaming the other person for their part in it. This is not always easy to do, but we have begun retraining ourselves in Steps 4 and 5 to take responsibility for our actions instead of blaming others. Through working Steps 6 & 7, we continue to develop insight into our behavior so that we can honestly acknowledge where we are at fault. There are situations where we have clearly caused the problem and others where we may feel hurt but see how we contributed to the situation. As our humility grows, we become more adept and willing to admit when we are wrong in both circumstances. As the Big Book says on page 69, "We must be willing to make amends where we have done harm, provided that we do not bring about still more harm in so doing."

Just for Today: Saying "I'm sorry" is different from saying, "I was wrong." We can be sorry and still feel we were right. But when we say we were wrong, we truly acknowledge our part in causing the problem.

July 28 — Being Right or Being Happy

The slogan "you can be right or you can be happy" is fitting when it comes to self-righteous indignation. "Being right" can wreak havoc on our bodies when we spin out of control with adrenaline trying to prove it to others; it can destroy relationships by diminishing the other person with criticism and judgment. So how do we move into "or you can be happy?" when we think our satisfaction depends on not just being right but on everyone agreeing with us? We get there by doing what we did with our debting and spending. First, we stop the behavior. And second, we become willing to feel the discomfort of not convincing everyone of our point of view, and seeing that we will not die if we don't. With practice, we become increasingly willing to release the stranglehold the idea that we must be right has on our ego. We don't have to let go of our point of view, just our insistence that everyone agree with us. But we may find even more peace in opening our heart and mind to the idea that right and wrong is not necessarily unequivocal and that there may be another valid point of view.

Just for Today: If you feel self-righteousness rising up in you, stay quiet until the storm passes and you can express your belief without damaging yourself or others.

July 29 — Fear of Creditors

Page 78 of the Big Book states that "we must lose our fear of creditors no matter how far we have to go, for we are liable to drink if we are afraid to face them." In the case of compulsive debtors and spenders, it is not the drink that might swallow us up, but a continuing pattern of debting and spending that we use as a shield against the pain of the truth. Fear is the dark and ugly weapon our disease uses to delude us into believing that engaging in the very action that got us into trouble in the first place is the way out of our problem. Many of us come into program with stacks of unopened bills and unanswered calls. Recovery leads us to the truth that there is nothing a creditor can do to us that is worse than what the imagined monster we have conjured up has already done in our minds. We learn that we do not have to accept abuse from our creditors nor do we allow ourselves to be intimidated into a commitment we cannot keep. With recovery, we learn integrity around our promises for repayment, even if that means we must admit to our creditors that we can pay nothing at this time, knowing that this will eventually change if we stay abstinent.

Just for Today: We do not have to fear our creditors. We have the power of the program, our Higher Power, and our network to support us.

July 30   The Race to Hit Bottom

Some compulsive debtors and spenders hit their bottom when they discover they can't earn their way out of their addiction. Even with two or three jobs, once the debt is paid off, their trigger-happy fingers can't keep from whipping out the charge cards once again. How many times did we pay off our credit cards and swear we would never accrue more than we could pay back in full each month, only to find ourselves drowning in debt in short order. Unconsciously, we ran ourselves ragged trying to feed an insatiable appetite.

Some of us didn't have debt, but engaged in a lifestyle that required that same level of overworking to maintain it, never seeing that we were too busy to enjoy the "stuff" we worked so hard to buy. We also ignored the toll overworking took on our health and our relationships as our children grew older and our partners more distant.

It is a great miracle when someone finally hits bottom and seeks out the D.A. program. Out of this complete demoralization, the compulsive debtor and spender has a remarkable opportunity to re-start, and live a conscious, joyful, balanced life.

Just for Today: How lucky we are to have hit the bottom that brought us to D.A. and recovery.

July 31 — Sisterly/Brother Love

Love of others brings us far more inner peace than hatred does. When we acknowledge that others are no different than we are, no more fallible and filled with defects, then we can forgive them their trespasses with compassion. Or at least we can try.

Too often, we criticize, judge, and romance our dislike for others. When we find ourselves doing that, we can take a breath and think about the fact that these are just other humans doing their best, even if their best is causing us harm.

This principle is best expressed through the slogan, "principles, before personalities" within 12 Step Fellowships. We need each other more than we need to find fault with any particular member. Practicing sisterly/brotherly love with difficult personalities can shift our judgment and takes us out of our own ego-driven perceptions. We are never going to like everyone we meet. But we can love the humanity within them.

Just for Today: Aspiring to love is all it takes. We just have to try. That's all.

August 1 — Forgive and Forget

Forgiveness helps us release resentment, but it doesn't necessarily mean reconciliation. What does it mean when we say that we forgive, but we don't forget? If we keep remembering, then we stoke the flames of resentment. On the other hand, it may be a matter of personal safety to remember. So in this case, remembering can be cradled in compassion. Compassion allows us to have understanding concern while we keep our distance. Forgiveness can sometimes be used as a way to make us feel that we are better than others, as if we are the beneficent faultless bestowing grace on the less fortunate flawed. Compassion equalizes and reminds us that we, too, are imperfect. Most of us have had our trespasses forgiven by another at one time or other, but how did we feel when people said they forgave us but used any excuse to remind us of their "not forgetting?" Is that really what we're trying to achieve? Maybe it is altogether better for us to aspire to compassion rather than forgiveness if we want to live in peace.

Just for Today: If we want to be truly free, it is clear that we cannot use forgiveness as a weapon.

August 2 — Jealousy and Envy

It becomes clear as we work the steps that comparison is just another way to cause ourselves harm. In recovery, we begin to keep our eyes on our own lives and our Higher Power's will for us, not what anyone else's path may bring. When we use the tools of our program to help us live in acceptance and gratitude, jealousy and envy will fall away naturally.

How blessed we are to have a program that can bring us peace of mind under all circumstances. It is only by working this program that we learn to get right-minded about jealousy and envy, and to see how unproductive it is to compare ourselves to others. We each have our gifts and we each have our trials. No one, absolutely no one, gets away with a purely gilded life. The fact is all of us eventually die no matter how wealthy and powerful we think we are in this life. So in the end, we leave this earth absolutely equal.

Just for Today: If you begin to feel jealous or envious, turn your thoughts to gratitude for what you have.

August 3   Regretting the Past

On page 83 of the Big Book, we are promised that "we will not regret the past nor wish to shut the door on it." Through the hard work of Step Four, and talking it through with someone in Step Five, we have worked on self-forgiveness, maybe even dropped some of our resentment, and found compassion toward those who caused us harm.

We now have spiritual tools to use for acceptance when we beat ourselves up for past mistakes (regret), but we also have gratitude for all we've been through because it led us to this recovery (nor wish to shut the door). This isn't once and done, but gradually, these tools of acceptance and gratitude are more and more integrated into who we are.

The work of recovery is to create our today in such a way as to keep us from regretting it in the future. In recovery, the past can be a wonderful teacher to guide us in how to live in integrity, compassion, and sobriety in each and every moment.

Just for Today: Can you see the folly of regretting the past?

August 4 — Dependence

In order to keep from making your sponsor your Higher Power, it is imperative to develop a network of people in program to turn to for support and to whom you can give service. Making a commitment to daily calls is the only way those of us whose tendency is to isolate will develop relationships in the program.

Remember, you are not the only call your sponsor receives and makes. And she should not be the only person you turn to in times of distress. In fact, you may even consider having two other people on your pressure relief group team. We can turn to our team to help us with big spending decisions and pressures, while our sponsor helps us with day-to-day choices and issues.

But the most important reason for having a well-developed network is that they will keep you buoyed up if you lose your sponsor until you find another. Yes, in a sense we are dependent on each other for support, but we don't want to become overly dependent on any one individual.

Just for Today: Have you made an outreach call?

August 5 — Active Reflection

After we ask for guidance in prayer and sit in meditation to receive the answer, we follow up with reflection to ensure we are not acting out of self-will. As the Big Book says on page 87, "Being still inexperienced and having just made conscious contact with God, it is not probable that we are going to be inspired at all times. We might pay for this presumption in all sorts of absurd actions and ideas." We can integrate reflection with action steps as a precaution for such presumption. In the case of spending, we can wait at least 24 hours before acting, no matter how much urgency we feel (for instance, knowing the sale ends today). We can speak to our sponsor about the course we want to take. We discuss our decision with our network, seeking to include those who may not agree with us. If the decision involves a large expenditure, we can schedule a PRG to create a spending plan. Writing is always a good idea because often more information comes out of our subconscious when we let pen flow freely on paper. Reflection is only possible if we take a pause before acting, but there is no way to reflect when we act impulsively. Unfortunately, for people like us, acting on impulse often leads to debting and regretting.

Just for Today: Try to pause as an integral part of reflection.

August 6   About Amends

We want to be careful not to use the amends process as a sneaky way to blame the other person. Sometimes, even if we want to take responsibility for our part, it can feel really challenging not to add that "but" onto our apology. But if we are sincere about making our amends, we will keep it to ourselves. Apologizing without changing our behavior becomes meaningless … like people who gamble, apologize, and then do it again a week later. The key to amends is both owning our part and righting the wrong.

There are two types of amends. With direct amends, we tell someone (preferably in person), that we were wrong, apologize, and try to right the error. With a living amends, we don't go to the person to admit our wrongdoing. Instead, we work on changing the defect or righting the wrong through our actions only. We may need to do a living amends if the other party is unreachable, dead, or if apologizing could cause more harm than good. So, for instance, we may contribute to a pet adoption agency if we were cruel to an animal or donate office supplies to a charity if we took them from a company that is no longer in business.

Just for Today: We keep our amends clean, knowing that the benefit we gain comes from focusing solely on where we were wrong.

August 7 — Obsession's Fallout

Our obsession with shopping or researching can take a toll on our relationships. Those hours we spend in the mall or glued to our computers are time that we lose with our families, and can add up to months or even years lost. We may sit down at the computer at 9 p.m., vowing to read just a couple product reviews and when we look up, it's 3 a.m., and we've gone far afield of our original purpose. Technology makes feeding this obsession so easy that we can engage while lying in bed, eating dinner, or even while talking on the phone. In recovery, we strive for clarity instead of vagueness. Distraction is vagueness' partner. Obsessive distraction can make us oversleep, miss appointments, and distance us from those we love. We now have an opportunity to change these patterns of behavior. We can bookend with others to limit our time spent researching or shopping online, for instance. We can make a commitment to spend a certain amount of time each day with our families instead of engaging in time-wasting behaviors. For those of us with children, changing this pattern is vital. First, our children need our attention to grow into healthy adults and, second, we don't want to pass on our destructive habits.

Just for Today: Limit the time spent feeding your obsessions.

August 8   Consequences and Forgiveness

The other side of making amends is truly letting go of how we feel about others who have wronged us. Usually, we call this forgiveness. But when we forgive, in some way, we are placing ourselves above others, as if we are the better person. But humility, a core component of recovery thinking, tells us that we are equal to others, no better and no worse.

The truth is, even if we "forgive" others, they still have to experience the consequences of their actions. We are not in charge of that nor do we have the power to alter their consequences. That is between them and their Higher Power.

Our part is to first work to release our anger and resentment at others and what they did to us. This is necessary for our recovery, for our spiritual growth, and for our peace of mind. The next step is to replace that anger and hatred with love and compassion.

Just for Today: If we can release our anger and replace resentment with compassion and love, we are free.

August 9   All Are Welcome

The only requirement for membership in Debtors Anonymous "is a desire to stop incurring unsecured debt." But anyone who has problems with money is welcome in D.A.. Debt is often the final result of compulsive spending or underearning, and some of us find recovery before reaching the point of debting or after paying off our debt but as we are making our way back to it again. Others may have plenty of money, but their compulsive spending has made their lives unmanageable. Some may have no debt, but are terrified of what will happen if they spend their money on anything but the barest of necessities. These people find their way to the program when they hit a bottom that may have nothing to do with debt, but with the quality of their lives. With or without debt, D.A. teaches those who choose recovery how to be right-minded about money and how to live a balanced life financially, emotionally, and spiritually.

Just for Today: Anyone who says he or she is a member of D.A. is a member. We all share the common desire to keep from incurring unsecured debt one day at a time no matter how else our challenges with money manifest.

August 10 — Spending Moratorium

Even after we've been abstinent in program for a while, we may find that we continue to feel compulsive around spending in one or more categories. For some, it may be clothing, for others, crafts supplies or books. But any discretionary category may cause the disturbance. We compulsively spend every penny early in the month and obsess the rest of the month over what we'll buy next. Maybe we even want to accumulate money in this category, but month after month, we find items that we simply "can't live without," so saving for a purchase feels impossible. In such a case, we may consider a spending moratorium or holiday, which involves a commitment to refraining from making *any* purchases in a given category one day at a time for a period of time (often 90 days). It takes a great deal of courage and commitment to engage in such a measure, and we may be shocked at the degree of pain we feel as a result of doing so. But the spiritual growth we gain through this process are worth any discomfort, as anyone who has gone through a spending moratorium can tell you.

Just for Today: Consider taking a spending holiday from a category over which you still feel powerless.

August 11   Right Action; Right Thinking

We learn in program to recognize our defects and become willing to have them removed. Nowhere does the Big Book say that we are instantly relieved of our defects, nor does it tell us *how* our Higher Power will remove them. We may believe that we aren't successful in our recovery if we still have disagreeable thoughts and feel powerless over changing them. We know that action is the key to recovery. In the case of our defects, what action can we take? We may not be able to prevent ourselves from a visceral reaction of anger, for instance, but we *can* practice not lashing out at the other person *despite* our thoughts. We can use all we have learned about kindness, service, compassion, and responsibility to keep our mouth shut when we know that nothing good will come from acting on our thoughts and feelings. We have tools and people to help us work through unpleasant feelings and thoughts so that we can achieve "restraint of tongue and pen."

Just for Today: Only by taking right action even when our thoughts are less than ideal, can we achieve right thinking.

August 12 — Rigor

Unlike those in other Fellowships, we who are recovering from compulsive debting and spending must not only be fully committed to abstaining from our drug, but we must also be just as rigorous in another area--our spending plan. It is not enough for us to track our spending. We must also ensure that we do not spend more money that we have. For those using the cash and envelope method, that means they must be careful not to spend all their grocery money by mid-month, for example, or they may set in motion a negative domino effect by having to take money from another envelope. For those using debit cards, it is crucial that they keep their spending plan reconciled with their bank account to ensure they do not overdraw. For most of us, maintaining this high level of awareness means that we rigorously maintain our records and reconcile with our bank account at least weekly if not multiple times per week. While numbers and money are precise, people are fallible and we will inevitably make mistakes. So the goal is not to beat ourselves up over our errors thinking we are supposed to be perfect, but to set up a system that enables us to be rigorous in maintaining our finances.

Just for Today: If you maintain your records regularly, correcting errors will be much easier and simpler.

August 13   Anonymity Prevents Gossip

When we think of anonymity in our Program, we generally refer to not sharing what we hear at meetings, exhibiting discretion when running into members outside of meetings, being respectful of the messages we leave on an answering machine if it's not a "safe line" (meaning that other family members may hear the message). But some D.A. groups take anonymity a step further. They ask that we not reveal who our sponsors and sponsees are. Doing so can be a spiritual practice of respect, good will, and refraining from gossip.

If we keep this information to ourselves, should an issue arise between sponsor and sponsee, either can discuss their problems and feelings with falling into gossip. Such anonymity is a protection for all involved. For those of us who struggle with refraining from gossip, this can be a first step in understanding its implications and a way forward to practice such restraint in the rest of our lives.

Just for Today: Practice anonymity within your program.

August 14 — Literature

Most recovering members try to read spiritual or program literature daily to shore up their recovery. We cannot always make a phone call or attend a meeting, but literature can be carried with us wherever we go, and can be a lifesaving tool if we are stuck in a situation that is causing us difficulty.

There is a wide variety of literature we can read. We are encouraged to study A.A. literature as well as D.A. literature. Depending on our needs, we can choose to read stories by other members, instructions on working the steps and traditions, or the Big Book. Websites abound with personal perspectives that may provide tremendous spiritual support. No matter where we are, we are never alone when we carry literature with us. Literature is the voice of our Higher Power in print.

Just for Today: Read two pages of program literature.

August 15   Correcting Others

Some of us may suffer with the defect of criticism. In recovery, we may have learned to reign in overt attacks, but do we still make the small corrections that can slowly erode others' self-esteem? Do we feel compelled to correct someone when a tiny, unimportant detail is off in an otherwise accurate statement? Are we insistent on showing others where they are wrong in every circumstance?

Happily, as we grow in recovery, we become aware of how we may be putting others down to build ourselves up. Once we make the effort to stop blatant criticism, we may become aware that we engage in this more subtle method of disparaging others. We may no longer drop a boulder by way of pointed attacks, but when we belittle or correct unnecessarily, we are dropping pebbles, one by one. And eventually, a pile of pebbles causes just as much damage as a boulder.

Just for Today: As refraining from unnecessary correction as a loving and respectful gesture.

August 16 — Writing

They say that writing is an indispensable tool for recovery. As recovering compulsive debtors and spenders, we write down our daily spending. Some members write in response to a list of step questions. We all write our 4th Step inventory, and later, the list of our defects and people to whom we owe amends. Following that, some of us write our 10th Step along with gratitudes each day. But there are members who, after completing their steps, add a daily writing practice in response to readings from program literature. These members use a variety of program literature as a springboard for this daily writing. For instance, they may use D.A. pamphlets writing on a sentence or paragraph read daily. Others use the Big Book or Currency of Hope. There are lots of resources for inspiration.

Profound revelations about the state of our recovery can be the result of this practice. We can see how we've grown and how old habits that didn't serve us have been replaced by new ones that enhance our recovery. A few minutes of daily writing can also show us red flag areas where we need more focus. While it may not be easy to commit to this type of daily writing, the rewards are well worth the effort.

Just for Today: Try writing your thoughts after reading a few pages of program literature.

August 17 — Positive Pitches

When members share their experience, strength, and hope at a meeting, it is called a pitch. A request in the meeting format for positive pitches is a reminder to share the solution. In other words, positive pitching doesn't mean that we can't share our struggles, but the message should also contain hope, and speak to how we are handling our problems without debting. Meetings that ask for positive pitches suggest that this is the forum to share how we are working through our issues abstinently, whether or not the problem is resolved. For instance, sharing that our house may be foreclosed on can be a positive pitch if we also talk about walking through the fear and continuing to live by our spending plan to the best of our ability. If we are not turning to debt to solve our problem, any situation can be presented as a positive pitch. Positive pitches often contain statements of gratitude, which can always be found despite our trials. Positive pitches do not mean that we must present a rosy, pink cloud view of our life in order to share. It just means that we share how we are dealing with our problems without debting.

Just for Today: Present a positive pitch at a meeting.

August 18 — More

Many of us live in a constant state of acquiring. We keep buying more and more, but never use up what we already own. The issue isn't just about the constant purchasing. It's that we suffer from the "next bright and shiny object" syndrome. How many times have we bought a book and moved on to the next before even reading it? This is especially easy to do with e-books, which may become lost in a sea of information on our computers and mobile devices. Or do we have a stockpile of yarn bursting out of the closet but find ourselves unable to keep from buying five skeins of the gorgeous new yarn that just went on sale? Or take the example of a painter who may want to try her hand at sketching. But by the time the drawing tools arrive, before the box is even opened, she gets excited about collage, and feels driven to order a host of additional items. The cycle continues, and before long, she has a closet full of supplies and feels too overwhelmed by all her choices to produce any work. Acquiring can be a hobby unto itself. But it lacks the satisfaction of actually reading the book, painting the picture, or knitting the sweater.

Just for Today: Take stock of your inventory of whatever you tend to acquire and commit to using up at least a certain amount before buying more.

August 19 — Boredom

Boredom is anathema to addicts. We thrive on high drama and adrenaline. But when we put down our drug, we also let go of getting high. Though some addicts can handle adrenaline in other ways, such as through sports, others must release the need for speed in their lives in order to recover.

With recovery comes quiet times, which we may perceive as boring. Boredom is that state of being restless, irritable, and discontented described in "The Doctor's Opinion" in the Big Book. Wallowing in such a state can lead to picking up our drug again if we don't do something about it. Indeed, we may find ourselves spending money or shopping as a way to avoid boredom. But there is no need to dance on the razor's edge of sobriety to deal with these feelings.

In recovery, we are given tools to help us move out of that state without being self-destructive. We can make a phone call, attend a meeting, read and write, meditate, take a walk, read a book, engage in a hobby, go to a movie, or spend time with our family, all while expressing gratitude for our solvency.

Just for Today: The best way to overcome boredom is to get out of ourselves. We can do that by turning our attention to someone we can help.

August 20 — Creative Outlets

When we let go of compulsive debting and spending, a lot of time gets freed up. We are now filling that spiritual hole with right effort, action, and thinking. But even working our program and spending more time with our families will not take up all the time we used to spend using our drug.

How should we address the void? We may want to consider adding a creative component to our lives. Most people who do so report experiencing tremendous joy, inspiration, and a stronger connection with their Higher Power. They also find this outlet helpful as another way to work through life's challenges.

Creative choices are nearly limitless, with many low-cost options. Sculpting with found objects, collage, drawing, writing, playing the harmonica, learning a language, and knitting are examples of hobbies that require little to no investment to get started. Plus, the library and Internet are filled with instructional books and videos to get you started. Even if it takes a few tries to find something worth continuing, the process, itself, can be a lot of fun.

Just for Today: Why not take a few minutes to consider and explore various types of creative expression?

August 21   I am Not My Money

When we were compulsively debting and spending, we identified with our money in all its manifestations. For instance, we were only as good as the car we drove, the clothes we wore, the restaurants we frequented, the balance in our bank account (or the balance available on our credit cards). If those met our expectations, then we felt good about ourselves. Otherwise, we considered ourselves worthless. In recovery, we learn the emptiness of such a point of view. Surely, we have seen and read about vast fortunes won and lost in the blink of an eye. How could a person's true worth depend upon such fleeting circumstances? When we commit to living within our means one day at a time, our self-esteem grows by leaps and bounds as we shift our perspective and learn that the true measure of a person is not what they have but who they are. Sometimes, we may feel sad if our financial lot isn't as grand as we hoped (or used to believe it to be). But when we don't debt and use money as a drug, we find that we can hold our head high instead of feeling ashamed.

Just for Today: If we aren't our money, then this is true regardless of the balance in our bank account.

August 22   Two Slogans for the Storm

"One day at a time" is a tremendously comforting thought. When we first come into program, the idea of never using a credit card again may be terrifying, and the belief that a crisis will force us to do so may be firmly entrenched. But we can immediately experience the relief of not incurring new, unsecured debt just for today. As we continue to live life on life's terms, "one day at a time" becomes a comforting way to handle all life's challenges, and goes hand-in-hand with "this too shall pass." We learn from experience that these philosophies are a magical elixir. How often have we been an emotional wreck one day and the next wake up with an entirely better perspective? When we want to buy something that we cannot yet afford and the compulsion is burning within us, "one day at a time" helps us remember that we only have to stay solvent today and that "this, too, shall pass" ensures that if we don't give in, the feelings will eventually subside and sanity will be restored.

Just for Today: Each time we use "one day at a time" and "this too shall pass" to help us get through our difficulties, our fortitude is strengthened for the next time we are tested.

August 23   Emotional Rollercoasters

Addiction is all about drama and recovery is all about peace. But as recovering addicts, which behavior do we choose? Do we blow our problems out of proportion, hell-bent on riding an emotional roller-coaster?

We can begin to break this old habit by replacing it with problem-solving instead of wallowing in our difficulties. We no longer have to deal with our challenges alone. We have a network of people, a program, and a Higher Power to support us. The Serenity prayer can help us differentiate between what we cannot change and what we can, and our Higher Power can show us what steps to take to make these changes.

Living on an emotional roller-coaster is just another way to get an adrenaline fix. For many addicts, adrenaline is a dangerous drug that must be administered with extreme caution. So once we become conscious of whether or not our behavior will trigger an adrenaline rush with its attendant harm, we can make the choice to take the calmer road to clear thinking and problem-solving.

Just for Today: Before you get all worked up over a situation, use your tools to help you determine if there is a peaceful solution first.

August 24   Ask to See the Truth

It is sometimes difficult for recovering addicts to make decisions. That is why the best prayer may be to ask our Higher Power to show us the truth when we feel uncertain. It takes courage to ask for the truth when we want something badly, because we must be willing to wait for an answer before taking action, and the truth may be that what we want is not in our best interest.

Our Higher Power may not speak to us directly, so though we may listen for an answer in meditation, we also seek to be open to receiving an answer as we walk through our day. When we don't get a response right away, we continue waiting, knowing that taking action without clear guidance is usually foolhardy. Sometimes, the answer comes in an unexpected way, such as from an article we read or an off-handed comment by a friend. We might watch to see if we continue to receive the same answer in multiple ways. But even if no answer comes, that, too, may be a clear message … that this is simply not the time to act.

Just for Today: Have the courage to ask for the truth and the willingness to wait for an answer.

August 25 — Racing Thoughts

People often say they cannot meditate because their minds race. But they don't understand that many type of meditation simply involve the practice of moving back and forth between our thoughts and an "anchor" (like watching the breath or repeating a mantra). This is such a simple concept with profound repercussions. If we persist in a meditation practice despite the discomfort of racing thoughts, we will come to know what a powerful weapon we are honing. When we sit in meditation without running screaming out of the room because of all the uncontrolled and unwanted thinking we do, we learn that our thoughts have no power to control us as we move quietly back to our anchor without beating ourselves up even if we get lost in the "story" once in a while. This is a powerful weapon we can use at any time we are faced with a temptation to debt or an obsession to spend. Instead of using our racing thoughts as an excuse for not meditating, we can embrace them as a way to practice saying no to our disease.

Just for Today: Take some time to meditate.

August 26   Fear vs. Commitment

We always have a choice between commitment and fear. This is an important thought for recovering compulsive debtors and spenders to remember.

Many of us are terrified when we first come into program and are told that we must cut up our credit cards, eliminating our "safety net." At first, we follow these instructions as an act of faith. Later, we come to believe that the program works as we walk through each day without incurring new unsecured debt.

But inevitably, we will all be faced with financial trials and challenges even in recovery. That is where we have the choice between our commitment and our fear. Are we determined to live without debting or have we built a straw house that will burst into flames if a match is struck?

When we choose our commitment to recovery over our fear of the future, we have seen over and over that miracles can happen by turning to our tools, our network, and our Higher Power as a mantle to weather the storm that ensues when fear grips us and as a way for us to find a solvent solution to our problem.

Just for Today: Commit to living without incurring new unsecured debt.

August 27 — Serenity Before Prosperity

When we first get into recovery, we may expect instant financial rewards for our efforts. But we quickly learn that our Higher Power is not a genie in a bottle, there to grant us our wishes while we continue on our merry way. We have a lot of work to do first, such as cleaning up the wreckage of our past and developing a relationship with our Higher Power.

Serenity comes as a result of working the program because recovery teaches us to find joy in the life we have, rather than looking outward to acquire more, more, more. Serenity shows us how to feel peaceful even as we deal with the financial turmoil that may still swirl around us.

Material prosperity comes later as a by-product of the hard work of recovery. It is never a quick and easy road, and the fact is, some people may never acquire the material wealth they had hoped for. That may be a hard truth for a newcomer to swallow. But those who stay the course learn that the prosperity that is gained by serenity is a far more valuable commodity, and is available to anyone who is willing to live a life based on freedom from compulsive debting and spending.

Just for Today: The miracle of achieving serenity before prosperity is that we appreciate all the abundance in our lives, not just financial.

August 28   It's Not Fair

It was our lust for instant gratification that brought us to our knees and into the rooms of Debtors Anonymous. The inability to wait is an insidious thread that permeates the life of active compulsive debtors and spenders. Instant gratification is strongly related to the notion that we are entitled to everything we want the moment we want it, and "it's not fair" is our rallying cry when we can't have our way. Even for those of us who earned a good living, saving was impossible because we couldn't say no to *any* passing fancy. We were unwilling to live within our means, telling ourselves that it wasn't fair to be deprived of the current bright and shiny object that called to us. Using credit cards ensured that "it's not fair" was never heard … until the piper had to be paid. This philosophy puts us first, giving us a self-centered view of the world. The fact is, unfairness is a core component of the human condition. For every person who wins, there must be those who lose. Each of us faces disappointment, loss, illness, and death. There is no such thing as a life free from "it's not fair."

Just for Today: Living by our spending plan gives us practice in delaying gratification, showing us that "it's not fair" can no longer push us around.

August 29   Program Burnout

Service is key to our recovery from compulsive debting and spending. However, we must also use common sense when determining how much and the type of service to do. A single mother with two jobs cannot perform the same level of service as a retiree with few responsibilities. Unfortunately, there are people have left the Fellowship due to service overwhelm, sometimes self-inflicted, and sometimes the result of sponsors pushing them to do more service than they could handle. We work a recovery program to have a life, but how do we find time to live our new life while giving back what we have so generously been given? Many of us have jobs, families, or health issues. Still, the most important service we can give is to stay abstinent and attend meetings. Without sober members there is no Fellowship. Without meetings, we cannot connect and serve. If we feel burned out by the amount of service we currently give, we can cut back without feeling guilty. It's far better to do that than to get to the point that we walk away from the program.

Just for Today: Become willing to take an honest look at whether you are giving an appropriate amount of service.

August 30 — Giving Charity

As recovering compulsive debtors and spenders, our relationship with money is at issue. Therefore, how much to allocate for charitable donations must be addressed as part of our recovery program. There are members who believe in tithing, which means they give away 10% of all their income. Others do not ascribe to that philosophy and determine a fixed amount to contribute monthly. We must be careful not to let our ego determine how much charity we give, and we do not judge each other over how much we give or to what organizations. Instead, we each seek to know our Higher Power's will for us in that area. We all have a category for Charity, but some make a separate category for 7th Tradition, which is financial support given to 12 Step meetings. There are those, too, who accumulate money month after month in their Charity category without giving it away. This may be especially true for people who only attend phone meetings, where there is no basket passed around. Often, fear of letting go or donating to the right causes may play a part. To overcome our hesitation, we may want to commit to donating charity monthly.

Just for Today: If we used to donate hefty sums and can no longer afford to do so, we remember that we can give in many ways other than financial.

August 31 — Humility

Apologizing, especially when others have done us wrong as well, is not always easy. But remember that we only have to apologize for our part. By taking responsibility for our own actions, we are not saying that what *they* did was OK.

Remember the Golden Rule – Treat others as we want to be treated. Or, said in the context of amends, we don't treat others as we *don't* want them to treat us. Either way, admitting we are wrong can be a huge relief.

Being so attached to being right that we cannot see where we are wrong can have lifelong consequences. Moving from "being right" to "staying right" can fracture relationships that will cause us pain the rest of our lives.

Humility is the act of showing others that we are no better than they are. By making a list of all persons we had harmed, and becoming willing to make amends to them all, we take our place as equals among all and just as fallible.

Seeing our errors and admitting them to others in a sincere apology or making a living amends heals the soul and removes the heavy boulder of "being right" off of our back.

Just for Today: We cannot control the actions of others. But we can own our part.

September 1   Making Amends

Step 9 is often thought of as a chilling and challenging step that people want to avoid, just like Step 4. Yet, moving through this step can provide a greater level of relief and spiritual growth. As with Step 4, the sooner we move through this step, the sooner we experience the relief. In fact, it is on page 83, right at Step 9 that the Big Book reveals the promises that we will receive. Step 9 may feel difficult for many reasons. We may be afraid that we won't be forgiven for what we have done and will end up feeling humiliated. We may think that the other person has done more harm to us than we did to him or her. There may be fear of additional consequences for apologizing, such as financial restitution or jail. Any of these are possible. Yet, if we have worked the rest of the steps to the best of our ability and remember that making amends to right the wrongs we have done will keep us from returning to compulsive debting and spending, we know that we can handle whatever happens. Doing the right thing may not always turn out as we hope. Spiritual growth is not always easy. But those who have gone through this process before us will attest to the miracles working this step brings into our lives.

Just for Today: Trust that your Higher Power will protect you in the process of making amends.

September 2   Before We are Half-Way Through

The Big Book promises on page 83 begin by stating, "If we are painstaking about this phase of our development, we will be amazed before we are halfway through." Halfway through means that we have admitted powerlessness over debt; believe that there is help for us beyond our own limited control; turned over our will and our lives over to this Higher Power; reached deeply into our past to take responsibility for our actions; and revealed all the garbage we uncovered to ourselves, to our Higher Power, and to another person.

But by the time we reach this section of the book, we have also admitted our defects, are practicing the opposite of these defects in partnership with our Higher Power, and are going through the amends process with those we have harmed.

We have put in an enormous amount of effort working through the first nine steps, and now the Big Book is urging us to take a moment to reflect on all we have accomplished.

Just for Today: Do you see the results of your recovery program?

September 3   Peace & Serenity

Page 84 of the Big Book promises that "we will comprehend the word serenity and we will know peace." We used to think serenity was supposed to be a high. Now, we understand that serenity and peace come from an acceptance of life as it is, no matter what, and we learn to live without adrenaline coursing through our body all the time.

Compulsive debtors in recovery come to see how dangerous excitement and adrenaline can be – whether about something terrible *or* wonderful. We learn to prefer feeling calm to that racing feeling of anticipation or dread. We may still go for it sometimes, but our body and emotions pay the price when we do.

As addicts, we cannot afford to get overly riled up and excited, just as we cannot afford to give in to resentment and anger. In recovery, we learn that our choices can lead to an adrenaline rush or to peace. We can choose whether or not to rev up the engines when dealing with any situation.

Just for Today: Do you believe that you can face your creditors and debt with calm instead of panic?

September 4 — Distraction

Distraction has a negative connotation when it presents as a refusal to deal with our responsibilities or a pressing situation. However, distraction can be a useful tool if properly managed within recovery.

When experiencing an obsession to spend or debt, it is in our best interest to shift our focus. Program tells us to turn our thoughts to someone we can help. Withdrawal from compulsive spending and debting is a terrible foe and we need all the help we can get to move through it.

When we don't have a lot of discretionary funds, instead of wallowing in self-pity, we can distract ourselves with free or affordable forms of entertainment. The library is full of books, videos, and audios as is the Internet. Taking a walk costs nothing and is a wonderful way to clear our minds.

When life throws us a curveball, we learn in recovery to take the next right action rather than avoiding the situation. But there may be times that we need a distraction from an unyielding challenge, and as long as the distraction does not cause us to pick up our drug, behave irresponsibly, or "check out" when we need to be present, we can feel good about allowing ourselves the time to recharge our batteries.

Just for Today: Make a list of constructive ways that you can give yourself a break.

September 5   Opening the Envelope

One of the hallmarks of compulsive debting and spending is an unwillingness to face the truth of our financial situation. But when we put down our drug, we learn how to walk through our anxiety so that we can come to terms with our bills and creditors. Despite our dread, when we finally get the courage to open our bills, what a sense of relief we feel. No monster pops out of the envelope to grab us by the throat and we aren't dragged off to debtor's prison. Once we are willing to "open the envelopes," we can begin the process of cleaning up the wreckage of our past. This is true even if we can't even make a minimum payment today. In Step 1 we admit powerlessness. Nowhere does it say that we make it all right instantly. We begin by keeping track of our numbers. In the process, we gain clarity about exactly how much we owe and when it is due. There is no way to gain this clarity without opening the envelopes or contacting our creditors. With the help of our Higher Power, network, and program tools, we get the courage to proceed, knowing that courage doesn't mean we aren't afraid, but that we move forward anyway.

Just for Today: Before we can clean up the wreckage of our past, we must open the envelopes.

September 6 — Home Groups

A home group is a D.A. meeting that we commit to attending consistently each week and at which we do service regularly. Why is this important?

It is easy to flit from meeting to meeting, showing up but perhaps staying a silent bystander. But since recovery is about service, we must actively participate to the best of our ability. While we cannot give service at every meeting, by selecting a home group, we become involved on a deeper level with our program and fellow members.

People get to know each other more deeply when they hear each other week after week on the same meeting, and come to share more deeply in each other's recovery. If we tend to overdo and our ego pushes us toward grandiosity, having one home group ensures that our efforts stay right-sized. Certainly, we can give service at other meetings, but the service at our home group becomes our priority. Attending a home group is a first step in learning to make and keep commitments, often difficult for recovering addicts.

Just for Today: Commit to a home group and to doing service at the meeting consistently.

September 7   Business Meetings

Some of us find business meetings challenging because they can get heated at times, so we avoid them. But attending the business meeting for our home group is important. A meeting requires the cooperation and input of all its members to run smoothly. The business meeting is the place to bring up concerns about the health of the meeting as well as deal with functional issues. Even though phone meetings have fewer service requirements, there may still be issues that need to be addressed. Perhaps members feel the focus no longer works or the time has come to change roles, such as selecting a new leader or treasurer. In-person meetings generally have monthly business meetings. Phone meetings may opt to do so less frequently, perhaps quarterly or even annually. If we are experiencing a problem at a meeting, it is important that we attend and voice our concerns at the business meeting, rather than just complaining to our friends. Every member's voice is important at a business meeting to ensure that the group conscience is in force.

Just for Today: Make it a priority to attend the business meeting for your home group.

September 8 — Courtesy

We must not forget that civility is as important at a business meeting as at any other. We cannot let our emotions allow us to disrespect others just because we may not agree with them.

In a D.A. meeting, we strive to be loving and compassionate. We discourage cross-talk so that we don't step on the toes of our fellow members, and try to remember that we are all just sick and suffering people who meet to find recovery.

Unfortunately, when it comes to business meetings, basic courtesy is sometimes discarded and the gloves come off. This may happen even though a few moments before, all were saying the Serenity prayer in unison.

We all come to the table with our own baggage. But at a volatile business meeting we have a remarkable opportunity to eschew anger and practice restraint, courtesy, and kindness. It is easy to be kind when others do as we want; much harder when we don't get our way. But the truth is, it is never acceptable to be rude at a business meeting. Even more important than the voting outcome of a motion is increasing our ability to express ourselves passionately while maintaining our civility.

Just for Today: Bring the same level of courtesy to a business meeting that you exhibit at a D.A. meeting.

September 9   Budget vs. Spending Plan

There is a big difference between a budget and a spending plan. A budget is like a diet, set in stone, temporary, and restrictive, while spending plans are fluid and shift with life circumstances. A budget encourages deprivation thinking. A spending plan recognizes that in order to live in recovery, our needs and some of our wants must come before paying off our debts. But compulsive debtors and spenders may try to convince themselves that they will be fine putting all their money toward debt repayment, leaving them with little to no funds for entertainment or clothes, and surviving on a peanut butter and jelly diet. This type of extreme thinking is what got us into trouble in the first place. In recovery, we recognize that living in the tight grasp of a budget can lead to binging because we can only feel deprived for so long. D.A. shows us the middle way and gives us the tool of a PRG, where two other people can help us allocate our money in a balanced way.

Just for Today: We are grateful for our spending plan, which is our gentle roadmap to recovery from compulsive debting and spending.

September 10   Living Within Our Means

Living within our means is the bottom line for compulsive debtors and spenders. But this is not always easy. For one thing, there is the inevitable desire for something we cannot afford that can knock us breathless. So even those with plenty of money can find living within their means challenging. And there are those whose means are simply less than what they need to live on comfortably. Healthy people can put their efforts into earning more money. Unfortunately, those who are disabled are stuck between a rock and a hard place, because the assistance they receive is usually far less than they earned when they were working. But even under dire circumstances, we've seen program miracles occur for those who stay committed to living within their means no matter what. We continue to ask our Higher Power to help us, and work with our sponsor, network, and PRG team to figure out how to make our spending plan tenable. We may have to be willing to live less comfortably for the time being. Rather than seeing this as deprivation, we can work on gratitude and acceptance, remembering that we only have to do this one day at a time.

Just for Today: We express gratitude for what we do have and for our willingness to live in recovery.

September 11 — Conditional Recovery

There are no conditional rules to recovery. While those who are disabled or suffer with ill health may seek desperate measures to get better when the traditional medical community fails them, if they are committed to recovery, they do not justify debting for those treatments no matter how much they want to try them. And if we are committed to living debt-free, we don't confuse elective procedures with true emergencies. For instance, needing surgery for a brain aneurysm is life-saving. On the other hand, we may believe that removing the mercury amalgams from our teeth will cure us and we may feel a sense of urgency to proceed. However, we are not facing imminent death if we don't get the procedure done today, and we are free to go ahead once we have the funds to do so. The fact is, if we or our family are faced with a real life-threatening situation, we *may* end up debting. It is ironic that ours is the only drug that we may need to use to save our life, but in nearly all cases, there is another way, such as securing the loan with our mortgage. If we are serious about our recovery, we will exhaust all avenues before turning to debt, and if we must debt, we find a way to secure the loan.

Just for Today: Are you willing to do whatever it takes to avoid incurring unsecured debt?

September 12   Humility with Numbers

Ours is the only addiction that requires math skills to live in recovery. Maintaining a spending plan accurately takes discipline. The fact that most active compulsive debtors and spenders live in vagueness and disorder makes it easy to see why accounting skills may not come to us naturally. It may be a struggle for us to learn how to keep a spending plan. But once we do, we feel confident that we will never mess up. While numbers are precise and unforgiving, keeping our numbers is a process, and it is a humbling experience when we first come to see that no matter how rigorous we are, being human, we will inevitably make mistakes with our numbers sometimes. But we know that if we want to remain in recovery, we stay on top of our numbers to the best of our ability, and when we do let it slide or discover a mistake, we don't beat ourselves up. Instead, we do our best to repair the problem. While numbers may not be forgiving, our Higher Power always is. And any error in our spending plan can be corrected, either by a direct fix or just starting over.

Just for Today: No matter how badly we mess up our numbers, there is no need for us to feel humiliated about it because making mistakes is just part of recovery.

September 13   A Prayer for Remembrance

Dear Higher Power,

Just for today, let me remember the hell of compulsive debting and spending. Let me remember the feeling of constant craving when I was in it. Let me remember that my disease may mask itself in the delusion of urgency. Let me remember this especially when I now have cravings. And each time I don't give into these cravings, please let me remember what it was like when I did.

With love and gratitude,

A D.A. member in recovery one day at a time

Just for Today: Let us never forget what our life used to be like before recovery.

September 14 — Seeing Clearly

D.A. is a program of clarity. We need to be willing to live in reality and that means understanding that our money is finite.

We can no longer afford to just spend arbitrarily and hope for the best. For me, it's not enough simply not to debt. If I don't have a detailed spending plan, I can easily fool myself into thinking I can afford an item, totally forgetting about a fixed expense (for example, car insurance) that is coming up.

Some people create categories down to the smallest detail and others have broader categories. For instance, I have a separate category for groceries, restaurants, and house supplies (like paper towels). A D.A. friend of mine simply has a category called "Supplies" that encompasses all those items.

It takes time to develop a spending plan that fits your needs. But waiting until it is perfect to use it defeats the purpose.

Just for Today: Are you using your spending plan? If not, get the help you need to make it work for you.

September 15   The Last Thing to Go

All along the road to relapse, there are signs that our recovery is eroding. We may start to spend hours wandering around our binge store or window shopping online. Maybe we begin moving money from other categories or savings to pay for discretionary spending. Perhaps we stop going to meetings or make excuses for why we can't do service. And then, however our descent manifests, we don't reach out to our sponsor, network, or PRG team to ask for help before it's too late. Debting is usually the end result of withdrawing from the daily actions and new habits that keep us on the recovery path. What's so frightening is the insidious nature of this slide into relapse. Unless we are vigilant, we might not even recognize the signs of what is happening until it's too late. Taking a daily inventory is the best way to prevent relapse. While we cannot work a perfect program every day, we all know the bottom line of what we need to do to maintain our recovery. If we find ourselves becoming increasingly unwilling to do what works for us or reverting to self-destructive behavior that is on the edge, a daily inventory will wake us up, triggering warning bells and a big red flag so that we can reach out for help to get back on track before it's too late.

Just for Today: Make a daily inventory non-negotiable.

September 16 — Why Accrue?

Accruing money in categories is essential to the smooth running of our financial lives in recovery. Where we used to scramble at the last minute to find the money for annual or quarterly bills, we now experience no drama and pay these bills on time because we've accumulated the money over time. We also accrue to save for something we want, but that is a choice, unlike the finite timetable of bills coming due.

All we have to do to accrue is divide the total amount by the number of months between payments and allocate money to that category each month. Some people resist this suggestion because they want more money to spend each month. But this is delusional thinking because eventually, the bill must be paid.

Dividing our money into categories in our spending plan is the first step to living in recovery with money. Accruing in these categories is the second.

Just for Today: Accept that it is necessary for a portion of your money to go toward bill accrual each month.

September 17   Spiritual Practice: Not Spending

Though we do refrain from using our drug (debt), we must also learn to soberly spend our money so we don't run out of it, which is an additional challenge for those of us who are also compulsive spenders. For compulsive spenders it is not just debt that is a drug, but money and what it can buy as well. Day after day, we walk a fine line by commitment to sane spending.

It may be spiritually helpful for us to take an occasional break from spending money, just as some religions indicate the need for a weekly day of rest. We can do this making a conscious choice not to spend for that day. While this seems easy, it may evoke some discomfort if we are used to buying something every day. But there can be a palpable sense of relief and calm when we do so. In fact, we may already have days where we don't spend, but never thought about it as a spiritual practice.

Just for Today: We think about our recovery in 24 hour increments. So, too, can we consciously commit not to spend any money for just one 24 hour period.

September 18 — Self-Delusion

When we first come into D.A. we learn that we must rip away the veils of delusion around our use of money. We then discover that this is not enough. We must also get honest in our relationships and with ourselves.

We may be terrified at first because we have dug ourselves so deep into the belief that our stories are true, yet we come into program because we have hit bottom and know on some level that we have been living a lie. What a relief it is to finally get honest about money. What a relief it is to finally get honest with ourselves and others.

When we are honest, we are not deluding ourselves into spending money unwisely. When we are honest, we get willing to listen to the voice of reason inside of us that tells us to wait when our disease urges us on. When we are honest, we can see where we are self-serving and inconsiderate.

D.A. promises that "honesty will guide our actions towards a rich life filled with meaning and purpose." What greater fortune could we seek?

Just for Today: Doing a daily inventory is a powerful way to keep us honest.

September 19 — Thinking Ahead

It's true that recovery is about staying in today. We don't sink into remorse about the past nor do we float along future fantasy.

However, when it comes to money and debt, we do need some amount of planning for the future to keep us sober. Otherwise, we would never save for retirement, never accrue money for upcoming bills, and never plan for a vacation, car, or other discretionary items.

Part of being responsible with money is thinking ahead. We do this initially by creating a spending plan and dividing all our income into categories so we know where our money will be spent. As part of this process, we make a list of all our expenses. We try to be diligent and list all bills that we pay, including those that are due monthly, quarterly, annually, and sporadically. We then accumulate money to pay bills that come due in the future.

Remembering that we are imperfect beings, we may forget about a bill here or there and get surprised when it comes due. When this happens, it may throw a temporary wrench into our spending plan, but we don't need to beat ourselves up. Instead, we address the issue and move on with gratitude.

Just for Today: While we live in the present, we plan for the future.

September 20   The Source of Our Abundance

D.A. promises that if we work the program, "we will recognize a Power greater than ourselves as the source of our abundance; we realize that God is doing for us what we could not do for ourselves."

This promise brings us back to Steps 2 and 3. If we are sincerely working our D.A. program, our lives are no longer unmanageable due to debt or being out of control with money. We may still have difficult challenges, such as underearning or foreclosure or a lot of debt we cannot yet pay off, but we are now living in the present, not burying ourselves with guilt about the past or terror of the future. But when we live one day at a time, we can see that fundamentally, all is well in our lives in this moment.

Slowly, we see that our problems resolve over time when we live by the steps and use the tools of recovery. Each time we get through an obstacle abstinently, we will have more courage and belief that the next problem will resolve as well.

Just for Today: When we look back, if we are painstaking about our work in D.A., we will truly be amazed at what our Higher Power has done for us.

September 21   Rewards

We can look at the experience of other recovering D.A. members to see how the rewards of the program manifest. Some examples of the program working in members' lives are:

* They recoil as from a hot flame when they recognize the obsession coming on.
* They feel saner around spending decisions.
* They no longer try to find ways to spend down their savings.
* They do not respond in a knee-jerk manner when they see a sale.
* They are willing to ask for help when in the grips of a purchasing obsession so that they can be restored to their right mind before acting out.
* They do not stock up on items just because they are on sale.
* They wait until they have the cash to purchase what they want.
* They are living within their means.

Just for Today: Make a list of the rewards you have received in your recovery.

September 22   A Thousand Names

Some of us may bristle at the use of the word God in the Steps and the Promises. If so, we remember that the Big Book tells us that we can define our Higher Power as we see fit. Some religions have a thousand names to describe a Higher Power. We don't need to call our Higher Power God. But in order to recover, we *must* believe that there is some power greater than ourselves that can restore us to sanity. For instance, we can consider the group as our Higher Power or the force of nature or even the Big Book itself. But unless we are willing to let go of any belief that we are in charge, we will not get very far in recovery. In fact, we will not get past Step 1, which says that "we admitted we were powerless over debt—that our lives had become unmanageable." Unless we come to believe that we are not able to fix our problem ourselves and that there is something or someone outside of us who can, all that will happen is that we will continue to debt and spend and spiral downward. The bottom line is that if you are to recover from this hopeless state of body and mind through the 12 Steps, you must come to believe in a Higher Power.

Just for Today: Are you ready to believe that only a Power greater than you can restore you to sanity?

September 23   All Is Fundamentally Well

People say that all is fundamentally well in this moment, but what, exactly, does that mean? After all, we may still be facing a mountain of debt or other financial catastrophes. How can anyone say that everything is fine?

This slogan is about examining the present moment. Right now, you are reading this page. You are breathing in and out. That is all that is happening. No crisis is descending on you in this moment. In fact, it may be quiet and peaceful.

By becoming aware of "just this moment," you can embrace it. In this very moment, no matter what bigger issues may surround your life, you can enjoy the fact that there is no catastrophe. Maybe there will be in the next, but not in this one. You *will* deal with everything in its proper time. But just for this moment, all is well. This attitude helps us to see that we are not defined by our situational problems. We will come to know that all can be fundamentally well on a spiritual level despite what is happening in the material world.

Just for Today: When you feel yourself overcome by anxiety about financial or other pressures, stop for a moment, take a few quiet breaths, and remember that everything is fundamentally fine in this moment.

September 24 — Time

Time, like money, is finite. Time, like money, has no favorites, doesn't expand to suit our needs. And it is only our perception that colors whether we feel we have enough of either.

When waiting to hear the results of a job interview, time crawls at a snail's pace, but when we're on vacation, it may race at the speed of light. It has been documented that as we get older, it seems that time moves faster and faster.

We all know that there will come a day, a breath, that is our last, and at times it may feel like that moment is racing toward us. With that knowledge, we can either sink into depression and despair or be as present as possible in each and every moment that is given to us.

Just for Today: Be as present as possible.

September 25 — Temptation

The Big Book promises that if we walk the recovery path, we will find that "we are not fighting it, neither are we avoiding temptation."

"We don't fight it" means that we are not white knuckling our desire not to debt or spend. Instead, we are able to handle all manner of situations with equanimity. For instance, we find that we can go into a store and spend only what we commit … and do so without feeling pain or yearning for other items.

When we are spiritually fit, if we happen to find ourselves faced with temptation, or in a situation that used to trigger us, our recovery enables us to walk through it without relapsing. However, since recovery is a path, not a destination, it is likely that we may have a tough moment here or there. On those days, we *can* choose to avoid temptation. And many of us do what we can to mitigate potential problems in advance just to be safe. So, for instance, we may choose not to go into our binge stores just to browse, and we cancel email and catalog subscriptions if they trigger us.

Just for Today: While we can handle temptation when we are spiritually fit, some of us may still find it more peaceful to simply avoid it when possible.

September 26   The Past Is a Dream

The past is akin to a dream. It is no longer real. When we hold on to resentment about an event in the past, we are holding onto nothing, nothing at all. Yes, our past creates our future, with each action leading to the next. But the reality of that past event is no more solid in the present than the nightmare we may have experienced last night, which caused us to wake feeling frightened.

But how can we remember this when we are in the midst of a resentment? Meditation holds the key. When we meditate, we learn that our thoughts do not control us. We also see the ephemeral nature of space and time as the minutes pass by. Sometimes, our meditation session feels like it has taken hours. At other times, we may feel that we just sat down and closed our eyes when it is over.

When we realize that the past has no solidity, we can become willing to let go of trying to grasp onto our pain about past events and relationships. Pain from the past may reach into our being, but we don't have to wallow in suffering over it. By remembering that our present reality is self-contained, we can more easily shake free of the shackles of the past.

Just for Today: We don't have to let past pain ruin today's experience.

September 27 — Less Is More

A D.A. member said, "When I was in disease, there was never enough money. But when I am working my recovery program and feeling spiritually fit, there is sufficient money to meet my needs, even though I may have less than before." This is a strange paradox, but one which many of us have experienced. It is not really about how much money we have. It's about how we choose to use it.

In recovery, we take the time to develop a spending plan, thoughtfully creating categories for our money. We then live by those categories instead of our momentary desires.

In recovery, we live within our means, which means that our money can only stretch so far. But because we think through how we spend our money, we are far less wasteful so our available funds go further than before. And many of us are amazed at how comfortable our life can be living within our means.

It's true that when we get abstinent, our withdrawal from giving in to instant gratification is painful. But eventually, the joy of living within our means far outweighs the short highs (and long lows!) of indulging in compulsive debting and spending.

Just for Today: We remember the pain of spending more money than we have.

September 28 — Wimpy's Hamburger

I can relate to the old Popeye cartoon character named Wimpy who was famous for begging others to feed a hamburger addiction he couldn't afford. His rallying cry was, "I'll gladly pay you on Tuesday for a hamburger today."

Every time the piper demanded to be paid after I dug a debting hole too deep to escape, I reached out to God, swearing that I would change tomorrow if He would only bail me out today. I don't remember huge pieces of my life because I lived in the fog of active addiction, the panic of past consequences, and the fantasy of future abundance.

Today, I know there is no time or money to squander. I don't want to spend my Mondays worrying about my Tuesdays and my Wednesdays looking over my shoulder. In recovery, I do my best to make good decisions about how I spend both my time and money. I know that these choices affect the quality of my life now and in the future.

Just for Today: If I can't afford a hamburger, I wait until I get paid again to buy one.

September 29 — Relapse

Relapse is never the same once you've experienced recovery. And, conversely, recovery is less likely to be taken for granted once you've experienced relapse.

However, we don't have to relapse to appreciate our recovery. All we have to do is to remember what it was like *before* recovery.

An excellent Step 1 exercise is to describe *in detail* two times you were out of control with money. Include the events leading up to the episode as well as how you felt before, during, and after. Finish up the writing by describing the ways in which you felt powerless.

We can reread this heartbreaking account any time we need a reminder of what it used to be like for us. It has been said that the further you are from your last binge, the closer you are to your next one. Attending meetings, making outreach calls, and sponsoring newcomers are all good ways to keep the memory fresh.

Just for Today: Please let me always remember what life used to be like before recovery.

September 30 — Justice

People have been known to make an amends and add a "but" at the end, as in, "I was wrong to call you a jerk, but you really hurt my feelings when you didn't like my hat and I think you shouldn't be so rude."

Justice stops at our border when we practice this principle in our amends. Justice is not an excuse to cause more harm, but to act on our own sense of right and wrong. Justice doesn't give us free reign to emotionally wound others.

Step 9 is about admitting our wrongs, not wallowing in our pain. When making amends, we attend to the justice inherent in righting our wrongs. We don't play the victim.

Just for Today: We have the courage to keep our amends focused on righting our wrongs regardless of what the other person has done.

October 1 — Personal Inventory

Step 10 suggests that we "continued to take personal inventory and when we were wrong promptly admitted it." This is how we work the spirit of the 4th step into the fabric of our lives. By looking at our behavior as we go through our day, we keep our "wreckage of the past" to a minimum.

The Step 10 spot inventory is meant to keep us on our toes in the moment. With our increased consciousness as a result of sobriety and working the previous nine steps, we find ourselves capable of practicing restraint in the moment or, if we slip, the willingness to clean up our side of the street immediately.

If we continue to apologize when we are wrong and make the effort to keep resentment from creeping up on us by setting appropriate boundaries and addressing problems when they occur, we can feel confident that we are truly living in recovery every day.

Just for Today: Stay conscious of how you treat others.

October 2 — Benefit to Others

Page 84 of the Big Book promises that "no matter how far down the scale we have gone, we will see how our experience can benefit others." This promise can come to life well before we have reached Step Twelve.

Remembering (not shutting the door on the past) is a vital component in our continuing abstinence in D.A.. Going to meetings, sponsoring, giving PRGs, and making outreach calls are all ways we can remember, while helping others. Honesty about our truth is what allows us to be of maximum benefit to others, not putting on a "good face."

Someone once shared at a meeting that he was terrified when he came into program that his life would end up in financial ruin. "Now," he said, "my worst fears have come to pass, yet I continue to stay abstinent in D.A.." He said that though the events had unfolded as he most feared, his reaction to it was completely different because he knew there was a way through it.

It's great when we hear from people whose dreams are coming true because of program. But it's just as inspiring to hear people who walk through trials in their life and stay sober.

Just for Today: Do I understand that my life doesn't have to be "pink cloud" perfect in order for me to be of service to others?

October 3   An Allergy of the Body

In "The Doctor's Opinion," (page XXV of the Big Book), Dr. Silkworth states, "We believe, and so suggested a few years ago, that the action of alcohol on these chronic alcoholics is a manifestation of an allergy..." Some compulsive debtors and spenders reject the idea of an allergy of the body when it comes to money. "It makes no sense," they say. "We can relate to the mental obsession, but money is not a substance that we ingest, so how is this possible?" We know that adrenaline is a drug, a hormone that our bodies produce in greater measure in response to fear or excitement. A surge of adrenaline can cause our hearts to race, our blood pressure to increase, hyperventilation, and much more. Adrenaline allergy may be the result of a dependence or addiction to these intense feelings produced by our brain when we engage in activities that stimulate them.

Isn't that just what happens to us when we compulsively debt and spend? We experience an adrenaline high when we work ourselves up over the next purchase, a rush when we spend that money, and a crushing low after the spree ... all followed by a rapacious urge to repeat the process.

Just for Today: Do you still crave that adrenaline rush?

October 4   Consistent Daily Practice

Meditation is a practice the Big Book instructs us to engage in daily. Doing so helps us better deal with life on life's terms outside of our formal practice. There are many ways to meditate and the Big Book gives a few suggestions, but no rules around how to do so, which frees us to find the way that works for us, just as the Big Book encourages us to find our own Higher Power.

Meditation can be silent or vocal, seated or moving, musical or verbal, eyes open or closed. It doesn't matter how you meditate; what matters is that you create and commit to a daily practice. Those who do, report that they are more able to detach from the claws of their thoughts and feelings, to see them but not be devoured by them. As an example, through meditation some people have learned to explore pain as an observer instead of as a victim, and, in the process, actually found that their level of discomfort was reduced. Consistent meditators report that they successfully use these new skills when faced with daily challenges.

Just for Today: It is consistent daily meditation practice that brings about the benefits we seek.

October 5 — The Big Picture

When buying a car, people may focus only on the monthly payments rather than the total cost of the vehicle. By doing so, they may not realize how much they are actually paying in the end. But if they look carefully at the final invoice, they may find a higher interest rate or additional fees and services have been charged that they didn't necessarily want or agree to.

In recovery, we learn to read the fine print as well as look at the bottom line. We become intimate with the details of our finances as well as the big picture. We are no longer vague about numbers and costs, and learn to love our calculator. Finally, we get willing to ask questions of salespeople instead of feeling too intimidated to speak up. For those of us who have been brought to our knees by compulsive debting and spending, this is a miracle. While these skills may not seem romantic or glamorous, putting them into practice is crucial to achieving the promises of program.

Just for Today: Are you willing to look at the total cost as well as the detail?

October 6 — Magical Thinking

The Debtors Anonymous program of recovery can restore us to sanity around money. But our program is not magic. We take practical actions to ensure that we stay sober with money, such as keeping our numbers and living within our means. And it is true that when we are willing to go to any length not to debt we often find what seems a miraculous solution at the 11th hour. But if we want to achieve our visions, we cannot just sit on our laurels and expect fortune to smile down on us without working for it. Money is integral to living a comfortable life and most of us want to earn more of it. However, with very few exceptions, receiving an ongoing stream of abundant income or achieving worldly success takes diligence and effort. If we don't exert the necessary effort to achieve our goals, then we are just living in fantasy. Keeping our numbers and living within our means is the first step toward that goal. But in order to make our material visions come true, we also need discipline and focus. We can easily differentiate between a vision and a fantasy by looking at the amount of effort we are willing to expend to achieve it.

Just for Today: Are you willing to patiently put in the hard work to achieve a financial goal rather than steamrolling ahead without making a plan or ensuring you can finance it soberly?

October 7   Carrying the Message

Doing 12th Step work need not be limited to the fellowship of Debtors Anonymous. We can do service in the community in many ways. Perhaps we can leave D.A. literature anonymously in a store or restaurant. For those of us who are willing to reveal our membership, if someone mentions their challenges with money and debt, we can share our ESH and direct them to D.A.. Even if we choose not to reveal that we are compulsive debtors, we can still lend a sympathetic ear and share the wisdom we have gained from our recovery.

    Our fellowship is small but the world is filled with compulsive debtors and spenders who may not realize there is a solution for their problem. But, of course, the best way to carry the message is for us to stay sober with money. By doing so, we are not causing harm to ourselves and others and are leaving a loving imprint on the world around us.

Just for Today: How can you carry the message of hope and recovery into the world?

October 8 — Being Prepared

Recovery from compulsive debting and spending requires that we become willing to prepare. Many of us lived by the seat of our pants, paycheck to paycheck, never thinking ahead. But when we commit to living within our means, we learn to plan our spending.

The first way we do this is to create a spending plan and assign our income to categories. These include fixed and discretionary expenses, and ideally savings, contingency, and a prudent reserve. We think about future bills and accrue money toward them. We may also make specific categories to accumulate money for maintenance and repairs if we have an old car or own a house, for example.

When we prepare for future problems, we are far less likely to face a financial emergency that puts our recovery in jeopardy. But that means that we must spend time analyzing our life and financial situation. This is where having a PRG can be invaluable to help us figure out a solid plan for the present and the future.

Just for Today: While no one can predict all unexpected events, doing our best to prepare for those we can anticipate will bring us peace of mind and enhance our recovery.

October 9 — The Best

Some of us struggle with feeling that we must get the best money has to offer, whether it be technology, clothing, healthcare, art supplies, or just about anything else. When we live within our means, we can't always get what we want. Instead, we get what we can afford. Sometimes, we cannot afford to get what we want at all. And sometimes, we choose to save up to get exactly what we want. Either way, this is a vastly different way of life from our days of actively debting and compulsively spending.

Surprisingly, rather than feeling sorry for ourselves over this state of affairs, a funny thing often happens when we are committed to recovery. We begin to look for value rather than "the best" at all costs; we think about what we really need rather than just what we want; we develop patience to save if the item is beyond our immediate reach; and we experience gratitude for the best we can afford to buy in recovery.

Just for Today: Can you peacefully accept less than the best?

October 10   Finding Loopholes

The Debtors Anonymous Telephone Intergroup states that in recovery, we pay for services when we receive them, except when there is a written agreement. This can be confusing. For instance, medical credit is available interest-free to pay for expensive services over time. So is that debting? If we are going by the idea that incurring unsecured debt is our bottom line, then it surely is. On the other hand, many medical offices bill for services. This means that we get the treatment today and receive a bill in a few weeks. However, the difference is that we pay the bill in full when it is due, rather than making payments over an extended period. It seems more likely that this is the intent of the D.A. Telephone Intergroup statement. If we are serious about our recovery, we do not try to find loopholes to justify incurring new unsecured debt. We live on a "cash only" basis, meaning that we pay as we go. We save for what we want instead of buying it before we know we have the money. Isn't that is really the crux of the problem – that we habitually overpromised and under-delivered when it came to paying our debts, truly believing we would pay them off, but in reality just lying to ourselves and others?

Just for Today: Are you trying to find loopholes to excuse debting or spending you can't afford?

October 11 — Underearning

While the primary purpose of our fellowship is to abstain from incurring unsecured debt, underearning can be a symptom of our disease. As we work the program, we slowly and steadily increase our self-esteem, which helps us have the courage to seek better job opportunities and strive to achieve our full potential in all areas of our lives. Working the steps gives us clarity into the nature of these issues. Prayer and meditation may provide inspiration. We focus on planning and finding practical solutions to help us increase our income through our PRGs and in discussions with other D.A. members and our sponsor.

In D.A., we learn to take first things first. We stop debting and compulsively spending. We learn to live within our means. And then, the process naturally unfolds to show us the way to acceptance of our current situation and, if it is our Higher Power's will, the path to achieving greater abundance. The fact is, for some people, such as those who are disabled, achieving greater *financial* abundance is challenging. However, those of us who work a recovery program know that we can experience abundance in a variety of ways, many of which have nothing to do with money.

Just for Today: Make a list of 10 ways you feel abundant.

October 12   Insurance

Even in recovery, my addict mind is focused on what I want and need today, and I can think of a million ways I'd rather spend my money other than on insurance. Car and health insurance is required by law. But others are optional. Some, such as technology or vacation insurance are relatively low-cost and short-term. But others, like long term care and disability policies must be paid over a lifetime. If we are lucky, our employer may provide these items at no or minimal charge. But the truth is if we *do* pay for them and never need to use them the money is gone with no return on our investment. We walk a fine line between preparedness and comfort. Certainly, if we don't have enough money for food or housing, insurance is not on our radar. But for those of us whose income provides more than the bare necessities of life, it makes sense to at least consider insurance as a part of our spending plan. Buying insurance isn't for everyone. But for those who do, making the decision may mean a long-term commitment not to be replaced by some transient desire, knowing that insurance for life's unexpected events could provide for you and your family in ways you couldn't otherwise afford.

Just for Today: What are your feelings about insurance?

October 13 — Gambling

It's pretty clear that outright gambling is a slippery slope for compulsive debtors and spenders. But there *are* some D.A. members who are able to engage in gambling soberly. Even so, we remain mindful that it's possible for the adrenaline rush of winning (or losing) to push us over the edge so that we place more than we can afford on the line. Lottery tickets are a close cousin to gambling because we are still investing our money into a risky proposition that could trigger grasping for more with a high probability that we will receive absolutely nothing in return. But are contests and sweepstakes, where we invest nothing more than our time to fill out a form, really so different? Such activities appear to be less troublesome than gambling away our income, but this whole arena is really about fueling our fantasies of receiving abundance with little to no effort. It's not the gambling that's the problem. The real danger lies in our indulging too deeply in fantasies of being saved by a knight in shining armor (a.k.a., money). As with all addiction, the mind is where the descent into relapse begins.

Just for Today: If you gamble, buy lottery tickets, or enter sweepstakes and contests, have fun, but make sure you are right-minded about your expectations before you begin.

October 14 — Hoarding

When we refuse to discard, sell, or give away what we no longer need, it is not a problem … unless this behavior adversely impacts our lives. While we may not reach the level of hoarding, in our addiction, some of our homes became cluttered with the accumulation of years of out of control spending. In recovery, we may find it difficult to part with the excess. In fact, we may find it terrifying to even contemplate doing so or trying to sort it all out. But slowly, over time, we begin to see that letting go of what we no longer need makes space for more of what nourishes us.

When we come into recovery, we don't try to clean up the wreckage of our past in a day. Neither do we need to rush to clean out our closets or storage units. What may seem overwhelming today will come naturally in due course. With continued recovery, you will find yourself willing and committed to slowly and surely letting go of what no longer serves you on a physical, mental, and spiritual level.

Just for Today: Be kind to yourself, knowing that your recovery is unfolding as it should in its own time.

October 15   Why Do We Debt?

Spending our time and energy trying to figure out why we debt is a useless exercise when it comes to recovering from compulsive debting. We find it better to focus on the solution, taking the necessary steps to live a sober life.

In the past, some of us spent lots of money on therapy in the pursuit of self-knowledge, only to find that all the awareness in the world did not bring about recovery. It is only the action of refraining from debting that will stop the vicious cycle and those of us who are recovering members of Debtors Anonymous believe that only the spiritual cure as outlined in the 12 Steps can bring about the healing that enables us to stay stopped one day at a time.

Just for Today: Are you still chasing after self-knowledge as the easier, softer way?

October 16   When Things Go Wrong

If our commitment to recovery is dependent on getting our way all of the time then we will soon have a rude awakening. Solvency levels the playing field. It doesn't guarantee a problem-free life. When we are sober with money, we can then deal directly with our trials and tribulations, instead of diverting our attention into the chaos we create when we use money as a drug. When things go wrong, as they inevitably will, we can choose to remain steadfast in working our program. Getting sober is not easy and that tough and painful lesson shows us that everything passes. If we stay the course, we emerge from the agony of withdrawal into the sunlight of recovery. We have learned first-hand that all things pass. So when life throws us that inevitable curveball, we adjust, using the tools of recovery to aid us in dealing with whatever we must face knowing that we are never given more than we can bear, even if our ego tries to convince us otherwise.

Just for Today: When adversity hits, instead of wallowing in self-pity, seek to act on the guidance of the Serenity prayer to help you weather the storm until it passes.

October 17 — Change

Change can be frightening. But we can no more stop change than keep time from passing. The knowledge of our powerlessness can either paralyze us or propel us into increased presence in the moment so that we learn to appreciate and embrace what we have right now. Acceptance of change helps us deal with the slings and arrows of life with greater equanimity. Our peace of mind cannot be bought and no amount of material possessions will protect us from the passage of time *or* change. One way we can help ourselves experience more peace around these issues is to take the Serenity Prayer to heart. We seek to accept our present circumstance, rather than fighting our reality. With acceptance, comes a letting go, which enables us to be more relaxed rather than tensing up. We can then better assess how or if we can change our circumstance because intuition and creative solutions flow more easily into a mind that is relaxed and accepting. We take the necessary action to prevent or change the situation if that is appropriate. And if there is no action to take, then the wisdom of knowing the difference shows us that even if we cannot change our external circumstances we can always shift our perspective.

Just for Today: Accept that change is inevitable and fighting this truth only brings suffering.

October 18 — Lack of Clarity

When vagueness rears its ugly head, we must be vigilant to stem the tide, because lack of clarity can lead us back into debting. There will inevitably be times that we slip into vagueness around our numbers. But it is the degree to which we let this happen that can mean the difference between sustained recovery and relapse. The longer we go without entering our numbers into our spending plan or reconciling with our bank account, the more likely it is that we will make mistakes about how much money we have. If we let this situation go on too long, we may become overwhelmed, resentful, and simply give up rather than dedicate the necessary time to unravel the mess or even start over. Such thinking opens the door for our addict mind to slide in more negative self-talk, convincing us to sink into an attitude of "who cares." Once we go there, it is not much further to acting on the delusion that a spending binge or finding some quick credit will obliterate the pain and make us feel better.

Just for Today: If your numbers are in disarray, take a deep breath, make a call, and finally, come up with a plan to get your spending plan back on track. If you can't get started on your own, enlist the help of another D.A. member or a PRG team.

October 19 — Spiritual Wealth

In D.A., we talk a lot about financial abundance. Our visions tend to focus on monetary and material success. Many of us come into program for this very reason. We want financial abundance and security in our lives. And when we work this program diligently, many of us do experience increased material well-being.

But there is a whole other level of wealth that is less talked about in program, and that is the spiritual abundance we receive as a gift of living within our means and working the steps of D.A..

As we clean up the wreckage of the past and work with our Higher Power on removing our defects, we learn to love ourselves and others more deeply. We come to see that though people may disappoint us, we have a source to turn to that is ever present. And we learn that we can be happy no matter what is happening in our lives.

Before recovery, we lived in a constant state of desire, an itch that was never satisfied no matter how much we acquired. But in recovery, we learn how to be satisfied with what we have and release that constant need for more, more, more. That peace of mind cannot be purchased, but must be earned by working our program one day at a time.

Just for Today: Focus on gratitude for the spiritual gifts you have received from program.

October 20 — An Asset List

One important step in recovery from compulsive debting and spending is to clear out the wreckage of our past. We take inventory of our lives, accept responsibility for our actions, make a list of all persons we have harmed, and make amends to them all. It may seem that a lot of the initial focus is on the negative. Where was I wrong? How did I cause harm? But it is important to remember that through this process we are *ridding* ourselves of this wreckage. And, as it promises on page 84 of the Big Book, "No matter how far down the scale we have gone, we will see how our experience can benefit others." This promise hints at the fact that slowly, we are creating a life-changing, positive shift in our perspective, moving from self-seeking to a life of service. But to be of maximum benefit to others, we must not only look at where we can improve, but also take stock of the good in us. One way to do this is to create an asset list. It is not always easy for us to acknowledge our positive traits. But before we can truly love others, we must learn to love ourselves.

Just for Today: Remember that loving yourself is the first step toward treating others with kindness and compassion.

October 21   Taking Others' Inventory

To take someone's inventory means that we judge their behavior, appearance, or words. Similar to gossip, it is a way we may unconsciously try to make ourselves better than others, and it is a subtle and insidious form of intolerance. For instance, we hear a member announce at a meeting that she's going to borrow from her child's college fund to finance a vacation, and we make the judgment that this person is not sober with money. But, in fact, the problem really lies with us and our self-righteous attitude. This is when we have to seek our Higher Power's guidance. We may talk to our sponsor and network about our feelings, remembering that anonymity is paramount. Certainly, if we feel that the person's solvency is in danger, we may go to them and gently tell them of our concerns, but only if we are right-minded about our motives and if to do so won't cause more harm. In general, we try to be compassionate and kind about the foibles of others, reminding ourselves that we, too, are susceptible to all manner of self-deception and harmful behavior.

Just for Today: When we find ourselves taking another's inventory, we ask our Higher Power to relieve us of the need to judge.

October 22 — If Only...

How often do we utter the words "if only?" If only we had more money or more time or any one of a myriad of items that we think will make our lives perfect. The problem with "if only" is that it is just another tool of our disease to try to fool us into stepping off the path of recovery and into relapse. "If only" is dangerous thinking. It pushes us into that fantasy land that eventually leads to anger and resentment when we can't get what we think we must have in order to be happy.

Recovery is about acceptance of our reality and taking the necessary steps to improve our situation as we can. We may have visions for how we want our life to unfold, but we can no longer afford to live in fantasy and constant yearning. The truth is, when "if only" comes to pass the relief we experience is "only" temporary. Until we become willing to let go of the magical thinking that something outside ourselves is the key to our contentment, we will suffer from the pain that "if only" rains down on us.

Just for Today: If you find yourself thinking "if only," turn your mind to gratitude for all you have instead of indulging in the delusion that this one last thing is the key to your eternal happiness.

October 23 — Disappointment

Even within the fellowship, it is unreasonable to expect that our sponsor, PRG team, or other recovering members will never let us down. We are all just walking the path of sobriety with money, working toward the reduction of our character defects, and increasing our service to others, none of which means that we will become perfect. Knowing this, we can work on becoming more spiritually fit in order to help us better deal with disappointment when it happens. By enhancing our prayer and meditation, by working on strengthening our relationship with our Higher Power, we learn to automatically turn to this Power for aid and comfort when we cannot get it from others or when they hurt us. We also work on increasing our compassion and decreasing our habit of taking others' behavior personally. So often, when someone lashes out, it has almost nothing to do with the object of their anger and everything to do with the suffering of the person expressing the anger. Remember, our addiction is cunning, baffling, and powerful, and we know from our own experience how we, too, may hurt others as an unfortunate by-product of our own pain.

Just for Today: As you go through your day, begin to practice talking to your Higher Power as if speaking with a dear friend.

October 24   Getting Out of Your Head

Romancing our drug can keep us stuck, or worse, lure us into the insanity of relapse. Incessant internal chatter about what we want to buy does nothing to move us forward on the recovery path. Therefore, it is suggested that we get out of our head to keep from going out of our mind. A first step toward changing this pattern is to simply get up out of the chair or bed. Make a phone call, offer help to someone, take a walk, watch a movie, or engage in a hobby you enjoy. Distraction is not always a bad thing if used productively. It can help us move through grief and longing.

If we are to recover, it is essential that we break the habit of debting and compulsively spending, not just in the world, but inside our own head. It isn't enough to just tell ourselves to stop ruminating because our minds will revert to the old thoughts (sooner rather than later) if we do nothing to replace them. Therefore, we engage both our mind and our body in activity that is conducive to our recovery until the new productive habits replace our old destructive thinking.

Just for Today: Distract yourself from your problems with some lighthearted fun.

October 25 — Failure

The word failure is fraught with angst and ruination. It's as if such a concept is a rare event instead of a common outcome. And as addicts, we may even extend the meaning of the word to how we feel when our desire for instant gratification isn't satisfied. Everyone experiences failure. It's how we handle it that can make or break our recovery. For instance, we start a business that goes under; we make a poor investment decision; we don't get the job we want. In these circumstances, how do we react? Do we beat ourselves up for making the effort? Do we mercilessly engage in self-blame? Do we vow never to take a chance again? Or do we dust ourselves off and sort out what happened to help us achieve better outcomes in future endeavors? D.A. teaches us how to use our analytical minds. We must, or we would never be able to create and maintain a spending plan or write a 4th step, in which we learn how to discern and take responsibility for our actions. Indeed, we now have the tools to turn failure into a learning and growth opportunity. Once we accept that failure, even in recovery, is inevitable, we can work on our attitude to help us use even this difficult circumstance as an aid to a successful life in recovery.

Just for Today: Can you accept that you will fail periodically?

October 26   Window Shopping

While they say that compulsive spending is just a symptom of our addiction, for most of us, the rush is from buying, not debting. That buildup of desire for something we want that we can't afford, especially if it's a high ticket item, but for some of us, even the anticipation of a splurge at the dollar store, can bring on a high equal to that of any drug out there. The purchase is that peak moment of desire satisfied, followed soon enough by a rapid descent into regret and despair when we finally come to our senses. But it is dangerous for compulsive debtors even to window shop. Spending hours in our binge store examining object after object, trying on clothes, or putting items into a virtual shopping cart online when we haven't got the money to purchase anything is a torturous exercise, leaving us dangling with unsatisfied desire, no matter how good it may feel at the time. We have to ask ourselves why we want to tempt ourselves and whether we are in fit enough spiritual condition to withstand the pressure.

Just for Today: Go to a store only if you have a good reason to be there.

October 27 — Beauty

We may get so caught up in working our recovery program that we forget to look around. Working with numbers, calculators, and categories means that we focus our attention on small details. It is appropriate for us to concentrate on our recovery and the steps we need to take daily to ensure that we don't relapse.

However, in doing so, let us not forget to turn our attention to the beauty around us periodically. Beauty can appear in music, art, nature, pets, children, movement. There is something healing and soothing about seeing, listening to, or engaging in activities that activate joy and peace within us and can enhance our recovery.

Each of us finds beauty in our own way. The key is to take time each day to seek it out, even for just a few moments. Connecting with beauty is a soothing balm for the intensity of our recovery work. We can then come back to our daily tasks with renewed vigor.

Just for Today: Consider what you find beautiful and seek it out.

October 28 — Laughter

Our disease is deadly serious. But that doesn't mean that we must lose our sense of humor in the pursuit of recovery. Scientific studies prove that laughter is good for the body, mind, and spirit. We are in recovery to heal these parts of ourselves. A balanced life that includes laughter is an important part of the formula.

We may find that our sensibilities change with recovery. Where we might once have found caustic or hurtful humor hilarious, we may now find it simply makes us sad or upset. This doesn't mean that we have lost our sense of humor, but that we need to look elsewhere for our enjoyment. Without our addiction clouding our world view, we might even find humor we used to think unsophisticated and childish tremendously funny now.

Our common pain, which binds us, can also be a vehicle for laughter. In fact, there is a whole community of recovery comedians who show us how our pain can be transformed into healing with humor. They do this, not to make light of our addiction, but because humor is a wonderful tool to aid us in keeping right-minded and having a proper perspective.

Just for Today: Seek out what makes you laugh every day and let no one judge your choices.

October 29   The Telephone

Whether for phone meetings, PRGs, or outreach calls, the telephone is a vital tool for giving and receiving 12 Step service. Sometimes, it feels like we must exhibit a Herculean effort to pick up that "1,000 pound" phone to make or take a call. We may feel scared of what others will think of us or believe that no one wants to be bothered listening to our problems. But recovery from compulsive debting and spending requires a team effort. Like it or not, we need the help of others to get and stay sober with money, and we can only get that help if we have the willingness to ask for it when we need it. When we do this, we often discover that the other person is helped as well. This is not to say that we must reveal everything in the first call to a stranger. But slowly, over time, trust can develop between members in recovery. Some members do get inundated with calls and become overwhelmed. So they must set up boundaries regarding the use of this tool in order to maintain their recovery. Therefore, if a member doesn't call you back, practice compassion, instead of feeling resentful. And move on to other members who are more available.

Just for Today: Remember that one of the best ways to perform 12 Step service is to call a newcomer.

October 30 — Enlightenment

Some people walk a path that they believe will lead to enlightenment, which often includes a practice of increasing kindness and compassion along with meditation. Those with this worldview understand that this journey may span lifetimes. Instead of feeling impatient, they find peace in the incremental progress they make each day. They do not give up when the going gets tough, but doggedly persist in their efforts to achieve slow and steady improvement.

We, too, use prayer and meditation to assist us. And though we may never be completely free of our shortcomings, it doesn't mean that we shouldn't persist in working with our Higher Power to overcome them. Every day that we increase in our ability to be of service to others and decrease our self-centered self-interest enhances not only our recovery, but the lives of those around us.

In Buddhism, they call the teachings that lead people along the path to greater compassion, kindness, and enlightenment, Dharma. For those of us recovering from compulsive debting and spending, we are blessed to have our own set of teachings that help us walk the path of recovery. We call them the 12 Steps.

Just for Today: Appreciate the profound truths embodied in the 12 Steps.

October 31 — Perseverance

In recovery, when we feel like giving up, we don't. It's that simple. There are days when it's easy and days when it feels like we're up against the wall. Sometimes people leave program when they feel the pressure to debt due to a real or imagined crisis because they aren't willing to sit in the discomfort while they continue to seek a solution from their Higher Power and the help of their D.A. network. Reasons to debt can arise in a heartbeat. We think: What if I don't get that training now? What if I don't start that health protocol today? What if I miss the sale? In recovery, we learn by experience that the more we feel compelled to indulge in major spending immediately, the less likely it is the right thing for us to do, despite how it appears on its face. Our program tells us to wait on all big purchases until the compulsion passes. Sometimes it is very hard to do, and those who choose to stay in recovery lean heavily on their Higher Power, PRG team, network, and sponsor to get through it. But the point is that we can get through it, and rather than the temporary satisfaction of giving in to craving and obsession, we feel the long-term peace of continuing to live a sane life in recovery.

Just for Today: Is your commitment to recovery only in effect when the going is easy?

November 1   Sought Conscious Contact

Step 11 suggests that we seek "through prayer and meditation to improve our conscious contact with God as we understood Him, praying only for knowledge of His will for us and the power to carry that out." As with all the steps, we are not only told what to do, but how to do it. Prayer is the use of thoughts and words to reach out and ask our Higher Power to become known to us in a way we can understand. Meditation is the means by which we listen for answers, and a method to help us become more attuned to our inner voice, which may be one way our Higher Power will communicate with us. The second part of this step continues to gently nudge us to let go of control. By now, we know that when we thought we were in charge, our lives didn't go so well. If we have continued to stay sober with money throughout this process, we have surely experienced some of the promises of the program, and we are getting used to letting our Higher Power be in charge. So the last part of this step suggests that we continue putting our lives in the hands of this Higher Power and just doing our best to follow directions. This is an encouraging step that doesn't ask more of us than we can give.

Just for Today: Are you willing to do your part in Step 11, which is to pray and meditate?

November 2 — Simple Meditation

Step 11 suggests prayer and meditation. The Big Book is quite clear on prayer, but there are no specific instructions on how to meditate. Though there are countless techniques, watching the breath is an easy way to begin, and many people continue using this method when they discover its benefits. We set aside time each day (perhaps 20-30 minutes), usually in the morning, to sit on a chair or cushion, and practice. All we need to do is focus our attention on our breathing, wherever we find it easiest. For instance, as we breathe, we might feel the breath enter and leave our nose or notice the rise and fall of our stomach. Once we find a comfortable focus, we stay with it. We do not try to control the breath *in any way,* for instance, by making it longer or shorter. As soon as we become aware that we are distracted by thoughts (and we will!), we simply go back to watching the breath *without judging ourselves*. Successful meditation is measured by our willingness to return to the breath over and over when we are distracted by thoughts. A calmer mind is just the by-product. Through this practice, we also learn how to sit with discomfort, an invaluable skill for recovering compulsive debtors

Just for Today: Practice meditating for at least 10 minutes.

November 3   Daily Inventory

Specific instructions are given on pages 86-88 of the Big Book for how to incorporate an ongoing practice that leads to spiritual growth into our lives. We are first advised to spend a few moments reviewing our day before we go to sleep, seeking to uncover areas of concern and how we can remedy them. The Big Book is careful to remind us that we are not to use this review as an excuse to beat ourselves up, but as a practice to help us become increasingly aware of our foibles so we can correct them. When we wake up, we start our day on the right footing by seeking the guidance of our Higher Power. By doing so, we are reminded of our intention to be useful to others rather than self-seeking. We are also taught what to do when we find ourselves "agitated or doubtful" throughout the day. It is astonishing how, in just a few pages, the Big Book has given us the complete recipe for a productive, useful, and disciplined life. But without the time we have already put into staying sober with money one day at a time, the effort we have invested in working the previous ten steps, and the recovery we've experienced from doing so, we would never be able to integrate this formula into our lives, much less be open to it.

Just for Today: We follow these instructions, mindful that we seek progress, not perfection.

November 4 — Grace

Grace is defined as "unmerited divine assistance" (Merriam-Webster online dictionary). Certainly, many of us believe that our recovery from compulsive debting and spending fits this description. While we may not agree on what constitutes "divine," those of us who have been restored to sanity around money through the power of the 12 Steps know that nothing else worked but admitting complete defeat and finally turning our will and our lives over to the care of a Power greater than ourselves. We were no more deserving of this healing when we received it than at any time over the years that we were out of control with money, wreaking havoc all around us, destroying our health and our relationships in the process. Being graced with recovery doesn't mean that we rest on our laurels. It does mean that we are given a chance on a daily basis to continue the work our Higher Power wants us to do to be of service to others. As the Big Book says, "We are not cured of alcoholism [debting]. What we really have is a daily reprieve contingent on the maintenance of our spiritual condition." Grace may be bestowed on us, but we cannot take it for granted. In order to continue walking the path of recovery, we must do our part each day.

Just for Today: What do you need to do to keep in fit spiritual condition?

November 5   Inventory Checklist

Detailed instructions on how to do a daily inventory are provided on page 86 of the Big Book. Many find that keeping a checklist with notes a helpful aid to performing this review. It's easy to create your own document to do so. Here are some suggestions for what to include. List all the days of the week across the columns. Feel free to add items that are giving you difficulty, such as exercise or meditation, for which you want increased accountability.

INVENTORY ITEMS
Selfish
Resentful
Dishonest
Afraid
Owe Apology
Kept something to myself
Mostly thinking of myself or others
*What did I do well
*How was I kind and loving
*Gratitudes
*Other (exercise, house cleaning)

* These items are not in the Big Book or have been modified to include positive aspects of our day.

Just for Today: Create your own inventory checklist ... and then use it.

November 6   Transferring Addictions

The only requirement for membership in D.A. is a desire to stop debting. But we might want to be mindful not to slip into another addiction once we are committed to recovery from this one. If we are in multiple 12 step programs, we may find that our active participation ebbs and flows depending on where we need to focus. This is especially true if we have long-term sobriety in other programs and feel that our relationship with our Higher Power is strong in that area of our life. But we must walk the tightrope of recovery carefully. If addictive behavior in other areas slips in when we aren't looking or when the pain becomes too great, we may want to look at the big picture. A commitment to recovery is the willingness to face life on life's terms without using a drug to soothe or mask the pain. If we find ourselves acting out with substances other than money, it is time for reflection and self-honesty. Of course, we may occasionally act out in self-destructive ways. We are only human and will inevitably fall. But if we see ourselves tumbling into a bottomless pit, let us remember how hard it is to climb out.

Just for Today: Are you active in another addiction even if you are sober with money?

November 7 — After the Storm

For some, the time *following* a crisis is the most dangerous to their recovery. We may really step up *during* the crisis. Our commitment remains strong and we are diligent in working our tools to the best of our ability even though the situation may constrain our ability to do so. And then, the crisis is over. Maybe the situation has resolved as we hoped, maybe not. But there is no more need for adrenaline to pump through our veins. We are back to life as usual or on to a new reality that requires ongoing acceptance. It is at this point that we may fall apart. The glue that held us together when the going was rough feels like it is melting away once we aren't experiencing that adrenaline high. So unbeknownst to us, a drug helped keep us going ... and now we are in withdrawal. For this reason, we must cling even closer to our tools and network *after* the crisis, *even* if we are bored or exhausted or sick of doing what we need to do every day to stay sober with money. We do it anyway because we know that if we stay the course one day at a time when our disease tries to sneak its way in, we will eventually get back into our groove and feel our recovery once again.

Just for Today: Be mindful in a crisis that the real danger to your recovery may appear when it is over.

November 8 — Pride or Gratitude

It is sometimes confusing for us to determine the difference between pride and gratitude. Both are evoked when we feel a sense of satisfaction about our accomplishments. But pride is like the blare of a trumpet letting everyone know how great we are, while gratitude is a whisper, a pleasurable sense of achievement while remembering the source of our abilities and the help we have received along the way.

While we must tear down a lot of our old ways of thinking and behaving in recovery, we do so in order to rebuild our "selves" into stronger, better, kinder beings. It is both wonderful and appropriate that we feel a sense of satisfaction with our increasing list of accomplishments in sobriety. But if we find ourselves shifting from gratitude into pride, we become right-minded again by remembering that we strive to leave our self-reliance and self-seeking in the trash bin along with the credit cards we cut up.

Just for Today: Take joy in your accomplishments ever mindful that you had help to achieve them.

November 9 — Slowly, But Surely

Many of us come into D.A. with significant debt. We may even feel suicidal when we consider what it will take to pay it off. Thankfully, D.A. steers us away from such thoughts and into a program of action to rebuild our lives. We focus our attention on not incurring *new* debt and feel a sense of relief and gratitude each day we succeed. We are supported by other D.A. members, who help us create a spending plan to keep us afloat without debting. At first, the mountain of debt doesn't move, and continues to cast its looming shadow over us. But now, a funny thing starts to happen. The mountain begins to shrink as it takes its place among the rest of our categories. Though we may still occasionally panic, we now see that the mountain won't devour us like a volcano ingesting a sacrificial lamb to get its money. It is suggested that we pay off our debt slowly but surely so that we do not deprive ourselves financially and as a spiritual practice of patience. For those who have followed this suggestion, the satisfaction of finally seeing a zero balance after months or years of disciplined, diligent, steady payments is one of the most joyous and fulfilling we can know in recovery.

Just for Today: Wherever you are on the path to debt repayment, be grateful for your willingness to walk, instead of run, to the finish line.

November 10 — Clutter

For recovering compulsive debtors clutter is not just a minor annoyance; it is dangerous to our recovery. Clutter is an insidious habit that leads to vagueness and disorganization. Vagueness and disorganization can lead to lost bills, piles of unopened mail, multiple purchases of the same item, and increasing frustration over the state of our surroundings. As clutter builds up, it can feel like the walls are closing in. Some of us are high functioning in the midst of clutter, but others lose steam in their recovery as their habit morphs into less rigor with their numbers and increasing disorder in all areas of their lives. Sometimes, we are unaware of the clutter around us (or in drawers or closets) until we miss a bill payment or can't find something we know we own. We may also suddenly "come to" and look around with dismay at the disorder in our homes. Clutter often begins when we leave the remnants of activities for later cleanup. One way to keep clutter at bay is to make cleanup part of completing a task. By doing so, eliminating clutter and the habit of creating it doesn't become overwhelming.

Just for Today: Start today to change a clutter habit by opening and dealing with the mail, putting things away when you're done with them, or taking just five minutes to straighten up a cluttered area.

November 11   Life's Small Tragedies

We commit to the path of recovery much like in a marriage, for better or for worse, in sickness and in health, till death do us part. But do we really mean it? We come into D.A. desperate, and willing to do whatever it takes to get out of trouble and out of pain. We may experience a time where things continue to improve. We may begin to feel comfortable and complacent as our life settles into a recovery rhythm. And then, one of life's small tragedies happens. Maybe we become disabled or our significant other leaves us or we lose our job. How do we handle our despair? Do we become angry at our Higher Power for not giving us what we want? And do we then question all the work it takes to maintain sobriety with money and decide to divorce ourselves from our recovery program? Or do we recognize and accept that tragedy comes to all of us in one form or another and that these small tragedies are inevitable in our lives? Do we take these opportunities that test our commitment to recovery and stay the course with gratitude and knowledge that this, too, shall pass? One day, the great tragedy will befall us or someone we love. Are we committed enough to recovery to maintain our sobriety with money in the face of death?

Just for Today: Examine your level of commitment to recovery from compulsive debting and spending.

November 12   Service List

Service to others is a foundation of our program and the key to staying in recovery. Many of us write a list of gratitudes daily to prevent our sinking into self-pity about what we don't have. In the same way, it may also be a helpful exercise to begin the day with a list of ten ways we may be of service to others for the next 24 hours.

No service is too small. So we may include such things as allowing others to cut in front of us while driving or opening the door for someone to enter a building. We might add a commitment to do service at a meeting or make a call to a newcomer. Emotional service, such as refraining from criticism, may be an aspiration for the day.

What we put on the list is less important than the fact that we are starting our day in a frame of mind that is more likely to make us feel good about ourselves. It is much easier to stay sober with money when we experience gratitude and increased self-esteem. Beginning our day by listing service intentions can set the tone for a better quality of life each day.

Just for Today: Make a list of ten ways you can be of service for the next 24 hours.

November 13   Defining Our Recovery

Debtors Anonymous defines recovery as refraining from incurring unsecured debt one day at a time. This simple action makes recovery sound easy, but debting is really just the final blow. It takes diligent effort on our part to stay in recovery. Therefore, we include in our definition specific actions taken daily or at other intervals that prevent us from reaching the point of no return. However, while there are certain common activities necessary for recovery, how we do them varies. For instance, we live within our means, but our spending plan may be detailed, or quite broad. Some of us commit every penny before spending it while others do not. We may live on a cash-only basis, keeping records by hand or we may use bank debit cards and software to manage our money. Members may work through the steps in a group, answer questions daily which they read to a sponsor, or formally work the steps only once and live by 10, 11, and 12 on a daily basis. We may write a daily gratitude list or a complete daily inventory or just think about it all. Whatever other members may do, the bottom line is that we are honest with ourselves about what *we* need to do to stay sober with money.

Just for Today: How do you define your recovery?

November 14 — Courage

It has been said that courage is not the absence of fear; it is doing what is necessary in spite of it. Making a commitment to live within our means takes a great deal of courage for compulsive debtors and spenders. Cutting up our credit cards when we first come into program takes a level of bravery that far exceeds mere courage.

As we walk through each day without the virtual roof caving in, we begin to trust more and more that we are being given what we need to keep our commitment to recovery, and we gain increasing faith in our ability to withstand the tough times without debting.

Our sword of courage slices through the false fears that our addiction throws up at us to scare us into submission and relapse. We are not without fear, for sure, but our sword of courage consists of tools to turn to, people to support us, and a Higher Power to carry us when the going gets tough.

Just for Today: Have you honed your sword of courage to deal with any obstacles on your path?

November 15   A Prayer for Hope

When things look dark, I often lose hope. It is so easy for me to forget that everything passes. In recovery, no matter how many times I have seen miracles happen for myself and others, I need to be reminded to have hope.

Without hope, it is easy to lose faith and then relapse. That is why gratitude is such an important part of recovery. Gratitude is a state of being that can bring me back to hope when all seems hopeless. Higher Power, let me turn to you and my friends in the fellowship to give me hope when I have lost it. Let me remember that hope can keep me sober when I am buffeted by the waves of challenges in my life.

I can learn to develop hope in the face of a difficult today by turning toward activities that enhance my recovery, such as reaching out to help another D.A. member and reading uplifting and optimistic literature, instead of wallowing in my misery. I can make a list of gratitudes and spend time with those I love instead of wallowing in my misery. Hope cannot grow in darkness. Just like a flower, hope needs the sunlight of the spirit to thrive.

Just for Today: We turn away from wallowing in our misery as a step toward renewing hope in our lives.

November 16   Grateful for Relapse

It may be puzzling for newcomers to hear people say they are grateful for relapse. No one is thankful for the complete demoralization losing their abstinence brings after a period of recovery. In fact, members often say that relapse is far worse than the lifetime of active addiction that preceded their coming into program. Because once you know the truth, there is no going back to a state of blissful ignorance if you pick up again. The truth shadows you wherever you go, even if you try to blot it out with denial and defiance. While they say that self-knowledge avails nothing that is not to say that a dose of harsh reality and the creation of more wreckage won't help a suffering compulsive debtor hit a necessary lower bottom. Those who say they are grateful return to program with increased willingness and commitment. Complacency and pride are two states of mind that can lead to thinking we can do this on our own. We certainly don't have to relapse to prove that we can't. But we do have to remember what it used to be like, what happened, and what it is like now to stay humbly grateful without having to suffer further.

Just for Today: Write about one or two of your debting or spending binges. Refer to what you've written when you need a reminder of why you are in D.A..

November 17 — Slip or Relapse

Both a slip and a relapse are willful actions in defiance of our commitment to sobriety. A slip is a single break of abstinence without repetition within a long period of solvency. A relapse is a continuing pattern of compulsive debting or spending. But what do we call it if we slip every month or two? A pattern of slipping may really be a relapse in disguise. Making a conscious decision to break our abstinence once is vastly different from getting back on track after each slip just long enough for the anxiety and shame to settle down before the obsession overwhelms us and we again lose our willingness to stay the course. In such a case, we have clearly forgotten that if we don't give in to the obsession, it will eventually pass. We each have our own bottom line that we cannot cross. Those who commit their spending consider it a slip to deliberately choose to make a purchase without first committing it. For others, crossing that bottom line may be the use of a credit card. It's important to remember that intention plays a role in sobriety. Making a mistake that you immediately acknowledge and correct is vastly different from willful disregard of your commitment.

Just for Today: Remember that it's easier to stay sober with money than to get sober.

November 18   Committing Our Spending

There are D.A. members who actually commit every penny to a sponsor before spending it, and consider it a break of abstinence not to do so. While that may sound extreme to some, this method of working the program has been life-saving for many members, particularly those who's addiction primarily manifests in compulsive spending and impulse buying. Members who commit their spending generally follow a few additional guidelines, such as daily reading, writing, outreach, and a call to a sponsor.

For those of us who work the program in this way, we do so because we are convinced that we need this additional rigor. We have found through years of trial and error that without doing so, we lacked the ability to withstand the compulsion, even when working an otherwise rigorous D.A. program. For us, committing our numbers is simply another tool in our arsenal.

We each have to determine, in all self-honesty, to what lengths we need to go to get and stay solvent. While not all D.A. members need to commit their spending, many who do find their ability to stay abstinent far easier.

Just for Today: If you continue to struggle with solvency, consider seeking a sponsor who commits his or her numbers.

November 19 — Spending Plan System

The decision about how to track your spending is best determined by you, and there are many options available. The envelope system is the most basic. You literally place the total amount of cash you are allocating for that month into a separate envelope for each spending category. Write the category name and total amount on the envelope. Every time you take money out, you subtract the amount and write the new total on the envelope. The challenge is to not only keep track of the amount you remove, but to note the exact amount of your actual purchases. Plus, a more detailed plan means lots of envelopes! But this simple system works well for those who can keep track of cash or are triggered by having a debit card in their hands. Those using debit cards may also manually track their spending on paper, but electronic options abound, including simple spreadsheets, online banking, and virtual envelope systems. The challenge here is learning to use the software and, for spreadsheets, ensuring that the calculations are accurate. Of course, you can mix and match to make a system that works for you. The best system is the one you will actually commit to using.

Just for Today: Is your spending plan system working for you?

November 20 — Consequences

We are told to live "one day at a time." But this doesn't mean that we cannot think ahead. In active addiction, living one day at a time meant that we simply gave in to the desire for the next bright and shiny object ignoring future consequences. In recovery, we are encouraged to think through the repercussions of what we want to do and have an arsenal of tools to help us tolerate delayed gratification when necessary. When the pounding desire for something we cannot afford grips us we can pray for help, reach out for support, or write about our feelings. We can also take a few moments to think through the short- and long-term consequences of our desired action. Perhaps we won't have enough money to pay our rent next month or maybe we'll spend down our savings, leaving us with little or no cushion for an emergency. We may try to convince ourselves that we aren't debting as justification for spending that we can't afford. But if we look ahead, we will see how the dominoes will eventually topple over leaving us no choice but to debt. It is at that moment that we can turn to our Higher Power to keep us in recovery and use the tools to get us through the discomfort until it passes.

Just for Today: Live in today, but consider tomorrow's consequences.

November 21   The Power of No

When we were in the thick of our addiction, we refused to accept "no." Instead, we plowed ahead, buying whatever we wanted, whatever the price ... as long as the credit held out. Now, we know that "no" can be a powerful balm to heal our suffering. While we may still experience a visceral reaction when we first realize that "no" is the right response in a given situation, our program gives us tools to make the medicine go down easier, including "not now" and "just for today," both of which can gently lead us into willingness and gentle acceptance of delayed gratification.

Often, when we postpone an impulsive purchase, we buy the time we need to extricate ourselves from the grip of our addiction's fiercest weapon: obsession, with its attendant feeling that we will die if we don't give in. Painful as "no" can feel, the reality of life in recovery from compulsive debting and spending is that we can't always buy what we want when we want it. Program teaches us to value what we have instead of focusing on what we don't, and we come to see that not getting our way will not only NOT kill us, but it will, in fact, increase our integrity as we remain committed to living within our means.

Just for Today: Remember that "no" is not the enemy. Compulsive debting and spending are.

November 22   Prepaid Credit Cards

As part of our commitment to recovery, we no longer incur unsecured debt. We cut up our credit cards and refuse all offers of credit, even when the clerk in our favorite store tells us that we can save 15% on today's purchase, and our addict mind tries to convince us that it's ok because we'll pay it off as soon as we get home and then cancel the account. We don't pretend that using a credit card for our monthly purchases is fine as long as we pay the bill as soon as it comes. Nope, we don't try to find a loophole; we just don't use credit cards anymore. But there are countries whose banking system doesn't offer debit cards, which puts recovering debtors who live there in a difficult position. Without some kind of plastic, they can't rent a car, reserve a hotel room, or make an online purchase. So how do they remain abstinent, yet function in the modern world. In this case the use of a *prepaid* credit card would be a solvent solution. It's a fine line, but if we fund the card sufficiently, then the money is available at the time of purchase. While this is the only viable option for those in a difficult situation, we must never forget that even a pre-paid credit card has the potential to be a dangerous weapon in the hands of a compulsive debtor.

Just for Today: If a pre-paid credit card is your only option, remember to treat it like a loaded gun.

November 23   Prison or Freedom

We can feel tight and imprisoned about our spending plan when we want to buy something we cannot afford today. Or we can sit with our uncomfortable feelings and recognize that we are making decisions about how we spend our money. Yes, we CAN take the savings we have miraculously accumulated in recovery and splurge if we want. Or we can breathe into the pain and reach out for help from others before taking an impulsive action that we might later regret. We can also have a PRG to fund the item over time … or help us let go of the desire just for today.

Money is finite. All we can do is decide how to use however much we have. And we can make those choices either in recovery or disease thinking.

So if we feel imprisoned, it is a jail of our own making. We have to make choices and in order to live a balanced life; we must recognize that we can't have everything. Yes, we can wish for more money. But would that really solve the problem? One thing I know for sure is that if you gave me one million dollars, I would most definitely need one million and one.

Just for Today: Do I really want to negate all that has brought me to this place of recovery just to satisfy a temporary, painful itch?

November 24 — Thanksgiving Acrostic

Going to ANY length not to incur new unsecured debt.

Recoiling as from a hot flame at the mention of Black Friday sales.

Awareness that this is a time of year where stores try to inflame my disease.

Taking time to meditate and connect with my Higher Power.

Embracing those I love at Thanksgiving dinner, even those who are challenging, with a loving, compassionate heart.

Focusing on seeing the good in my life today.

Understanding that everything can't always go my way nor can I control anyone else's actions but my own.

Letting go of my resentments just for today and allowing myself to feel the relief that brings.

November 25   Thanksgiving Gratitude

In D.A. recovery, we strive for gratitude every day. Seeking to find within ourselves, and expressing, gratitude is an integral part of all 12 Step programs.

The D.A. promises state that "Acceptance and Gratitude will replace regret, self-pity, and longing." Many of us who have been through the steps do a daily 10th Step, and list our gratitudes as part of that process to remind ourselves that we are reaping the benefits of our spiritual work no matter what other difficulties we may encounter. But we don't have to wait until we formally do our 10th Step to begin this practice. By writing our gratitudes daily, we will soon find that we have established the habit of looking at the glass as half full, instead of half empty, even when the going gets tough.

Just for Today: If you have not yet established the practice of listing gratitudes daily, today is a great day to start.

November 26   A New Way to Live

For me, it's just easier to ignore Black Friday and go about my life today; to deliberately NOT buy into that great "deal of a lifetime" thinking; to spend today doing other things in my life. Whatever I want will still be there next week or next month.

In recovery, we learn how not to live by the deal, and to buy what we need as we need it and can afford it, deal, or no deal. Sometimes, I've found that chasing the sale just causes me angst. Much of the time, the money I've saved isn't worth the frustration I experience doing all that's required for the savings (like "free shipping" when I spend over a certain amount, which may mean spending more than I intended).

Just for Today: You can use self-restraint as a spiritual practice for your recovery. So just for this one year, why not make it easy on yourself and your recovery by ignoring Black Friday?

November 27   Practice

Just as coming back to the breath in meditation is a practice, so, too, we engage in a practice by continually not acting out on our defects, and eventually, the emotional upheaval they cause is lessened, and sometimes removed, by our Higher Power.

Meditation is a microcosm of the work we do on our defects. Many people proclaim they cannot meditate because their minds are too active. But this is *exactly* the practice of meditation. We engage in meditation practice by coming back to the breath from thoughts over and over and over. If you have no thoughts, there is no practice!

Focusing on the goal of stillness will only cause suffering if you cannot reach it. If stillness comes, great. But meditation is an active practice of coming back to the object of meditation from thoughts, whether the object is the breath, a word, phrase, or prayer, a candle, music, or simply being in silence. By sitting in silence while we practice, even if it is uncomfortable, we are learning invaluable skills to take into our work on our defects.

Just for Today: Think of meditating as gentle action, and develop a compassionate attitude about the process because all minds think. That is what they do.

November 28   Fit Spiritual Condition

Spiritual fitness might be defined as an ease with living in recovery even in the face of challenges. Unfortunately, we may sometimes revert to old behaviors, which make living in recovery difficult even in good times. Continuing to gnaw at our spiritual fitness with such conduct will eventually lead to relapse if not checked. Nursing a resentment or exhibiting self-righteous indignation are overt examples of such dangerous behaviors. But there are more subtle ways we can find our program eroding without realizing it. For instance, maybe we decide to download a pirated copy of music or a movie when we have been diligent in our commitment to pay for our entertainment. Or we might begin to slip into gossip after being conscientious about not doing so. On page 60, the Big Book acknowledges that we aren't saints, adding, "The point is, that we are willing to grow along spiritual lines." The key is that we catch ourselves before we suffer a full-blown relapse. The best way to become more self-aware is by diligently working the steps and following the advice given on pages 86-88 of the Big Book for how to keep in fit spiritual condition on a daily basis.

Just for Today: Re-read pages 86-88 of the Big Book.

November 29   Weathering the Storm

Life is like the weather. There are gorgeous days without a cloud in the sky and times where a storm rages seemingly without end. How we handle the storm is a measure of our spiritual fitness. We can do it kicking and screaming about how unfair it is that rain is pounding down or we can strive for acceptance. In one sense, handling adversity in recovery may appear more difficult because we don't have our release valve of debting and compulsive spending to temporarily take the edge off. So assuming that we have not exchanged one addiction for another, we are just here, now, experiencing the turbulence. It takes practice to learn how to deal with pain constructively and without masking it by self-destructive behavior. But our commitment to recovery from our money addiction means that we forge ahead using all the tools at our disposal to help us do so. And we are surprised to find that our willingness to bear the discomfort in the midst of the storm, no matter how painful, brings us a rainbow of peace, insight, and strengthened recovery when it is over. We are blessed that we are not trying yet another method of essentially white knuckling restraint, but are working 12 steps that can provide us with a raincoat, umbrella, and safe haven to weather any storm.

Just for Today: Remember that every storm passes.

November 30 — Spirituality

Ours is a three part program, physical, mental, and spiritual. While we must refrain from the physical act of compulsive debting, if we are to truly recover, then we must also free ourselves from the obsession and compulsion that can overtake our minds. We accomplish both of these miraculous feats by working the steps and coming to believe in, and relying on, a power greater than ourselves.

Developing the spiritual aspect of this program means that we practice the 11th Step suggestions of prayer and meditation. Gradually, as we do this day by day, we sense more strongly that we are not alone and that our reliance on this Higher Power is beneficial to us. We also gain the ability to withstand discomfort without self-destructing. By investing the time and energy to develop and increase our spiritual life, we become more open and able to hear our Higher Power's voice through others and from our own intuition as we make better and better decisions in our lives. What a remarkable gift.

Just for Today: Spend time cultivating the sacred and divine spark within you.

December 1   Service

No matter how dark our situation appears to us, if we can manage to reach out to another person, we will inevitably find a bit of release from our own pain and often discover that the other person has benefited from our outreach as well. If we can not only bring our own issues to the table but also ask about, and actively listen to, the other person, we will be taking our mind off our own problems for just a few minutes, which may be exactly what we need to begin making our way out of the black hole so we can see some light again. In addition, giving support to someone else is a way we feed ourselves positive self-talk, a conscious reminder of what we know subconsciously.

Yes, we need to give back what we have been given, but most of us still want to know what's in it for us. So we may give service because it's part of the program, but what's in it for us is that we will feel better about ourselves and are more likely to stay sober with money because of it. Habits are created by repetition. Service to others is a good habit to cultivate. Working the steps and living by the principles of the program, such as giving service, will, over time, help us to live a more meaningful life. And isn't that what we all want?

Just for Today: Take one action to spread the message.

December 2   The Help We Need

Page 84 of the Big Book promises that "we will suddenly realize that God is doing for us what we could not do for ourselves." This takes us back to Step Two, when we came to believe that there was a Power greater than ourselves who could restore us to sanity. They use the word God here, but you could substitute the Group or whatever has worked for you until now as a Higher Power. And indeed, you can look with awe at the state of your life today because of this Higher Power.

Have you stopped incurring new unsecured debt? Have you given up compulsive spending? Are you sponsoring or giving some kind of service, even if just in outreach calls or at meetings? Are you working the Steps whole-heartedly?

If you can answer *yes* to these questions, take a moment to think about all you have accomplished *with your Higher Power* that you could never have done on your own.

Just for Today: Even if you are still struggling, you can answer yes to these questions by taking action today.

December 3 — Receiving Gifts

I have always found accepting gifts, financial and otherwise, extremely uncomfortable. As a compulsive debtor and spender, I loved being the beneficent giver. In fact, it was a drug for me, one that gave me a great high.

But receiving gifts, especially in recovery, brings up all kinds of emotions, such as the urgent desire to give back equally and a feeling of unworthiness to receive the gift. I have learned a lot in recovery about how to graciously accept such gifts and why doing so is an important recovery skill.

Accepting a gift, lovingly and unconditionally given, is also a present to the giver, and provides an opportunity for that person to express generosity. Accepting gifts graciously is a core D.A. concept, allowing prosperity to enter our lives.

Instead of thinking about how to repay the giver, it helps to focus on the concept of "paying it forward." Do what you are able, when the opportunity presents itself, to be generous to someone else.

Just for Today: Remember that we do not live in a one-way world. We are worthy beings, allowed to receive, as well as do, good.

December 4 — Life as Meditation

We can use the meditation process in all areas of our life to help us gain more peace. If we watch the breath as our method of practice, we can stop when agitated and just focus on our breathing for a few seconds. That may be all it takes to bring us back to ourselves. By practicing formal meditation, we learn that our thoughts and feelings, and even pain, will pass eventually. But there is no reason that we shouldn't have this experience as we move through life. It becomes more challenging when we are moving at warp speed throughout our day, but using our breath as an anchor, we can return to that state of presence in a heartbeat. When walking, we can use this practice to help us be more aware of our footsteps, and not just where we're going. When eating, we can bring in awareness so that we really taste the food, and slow down as we nourish our bodies instead of gulping our meals so we can get to the next item on our agenda. When ruminating about a problem, watching our breath can remind us that all is well in this moment, bringing a measure of relief. Eventually, we may fall in love with our breath because of the incredible healing it can bring to our body, mind, and spirit as we travel the path of recovery from compulsive debting.

Just for Today: Remember that we can bring this practice into every stressful situation that we face.

December 5 — Credit Cards

In recovery, we use cash, debit cards, or checks (as long as we have the funds available in our account) to pay for our purchases. Some people question this, wondering why we can't use a credit card if we pay it off as soon as the bill comes in or pre-pay and then use it. The bigger question is: why would we want to take a chance on triggering our addiction? Just like a knife, a hammer, or even a rope, a credit card is a tool that is a dangerous weapon in the wrong hands. Remember, it is the obsession of the mind over which we are powerless that can mean the difference between solvency and relapse. With instant access to our drug at our fingertips, we are more likely to pick up if tempted beyond our ability to withstand it during a particularly stressful moment, especially if we have an established pattern of use, sober or not. Besides, if we aren't pre-paying, we are receiving goods and services using borrowed money the instant we swipe the card, which is unsecured debt by any definition. Yes, the Big Book says that we are free when we are in fit spiritual condition. But nowhere is it suggested that an alcoholic bring a drink to her lips over and over to prove it.

Just for Today: Are you willing to keep it simple to stay sober with money?

December 6 — Sponsorless

They say we should find a sponsor who has what we want and ask how it was achieved. We then do our best to follow direction so we, too, can reap the rewards. But sometimes, we either can't find our first sponsor or we lose the sponsor we have and are unable to find a new one immediately. When this happens, members sometimes become demoralized and leave program. But the truth is that while we all want the ease and comfort having a sponsor brings, we aren't precluded from working the program without one, and we can still experience strong recovery until we do. In fact, members who have stayed the course have reported that their commitment to recovery was strengthened by maintaining their resolve during this difficult period. Without a sponsor, we can still remain solvent one day at a time, go to meetings, develop, and turn to, our network for support, keep our numbers, work the steps on our own or in a step-study group, and not debt. While it's true that the best possible scenario is to work the program with a sponsor whose guidance we trust, we must always remember that the most important relationship we cultivate in recovery is the one with our Higher Power.

Just for Today: Remember that it is our Higher Power, not a sponsor that keeps us sober with money, one day at a time.

December 7   Solvency and Health Issues

Recovering debtors and spenders with health issues face challenges not experienced by able-bodied D.A. members. If we are disabled, we cannot increase our earnings, and at the same time, we may need to spend more of the money we do have on medical treatment. There may come a time when we have to debt for a health crisis. In that case, we do what we must, but we are mindful that incurring any unsecured debt is a break of our abstinence and do not pretend that it isn't because of the circumstances. Otherwise, we may begin to justify all manner of discretionary spending for expensive or unproven medical treatments in a desperate attempt to find help for our situation. When we do that, our addict mind has found a wedge between us and our commitment to recovery. An unsecured debt is an unsecured debt, no matter the reason. In all self-honesty, we do our best to look for another way just as healthy members in recovery do. But if we must debt for a true emergency to save our lives, we simply accept the responsibility for our choice and move forward, doing our best to live within our means ongoing. We don't beat ourselves up. But we also don't deceive ourselves.

Just for Today: Disability can be a profound spiritual lesson to teach us humility, acceptance, gratitude, and letting go of grasping.

December 8 — Discipline

With all that it takes for us to live in recovery with compulsive debting and spending, we might laugh when we hear that this is the path to freedom. After all, we must keep track of our numbers, live within our means, place limits on our spending, go to meetings, work the steps, pray and meditate, sponsor others, and have a sponsor of our own, all of which requires discipline and focus. Some of us do even more, including daily reading, writing, and committing our spending. Yet, our willingness to do what we must to stay sober with money *is* the means to our freedom. We are free to answer our phones and open our mail, instead of living in fear of what they may bring. We breathe easier because we have the money to pay our bills and soberly make discretionary purchases. We are more loving, honest, open, and present in our relationships. We walk unencumbered in the world because we have cleaned up the wreckage of the past, and do our best each day to live with integrity and being of service to others. Finally, we are no longer enslaved by the obsession and compulsion that forces us to surrender to our every spending whim at all costs.

Just for Today: Be grateful for the disciplines that bring you freedom.

December 9   Solvency as Service

There is no question that being sober with money is the greatest service we can give. The whole premise of 12 step recovery is one compulsive debtor helping another. If we aren't sober, we can spout off about all the tools and steps, but it is the testimony that we share of our sober life that brings hope and faith in the process with another struggling debtor.

Without abstinence, there would be no sponsors because we cannot give away what we do not have. Meetings would have no leaders, treasurers, and speakers who testify to the miracles that recovery brings.

Our solvency, whether or not we remain anonymous to our friends, family, or the general public, enables us to be better citizens. We are able to lift our head out of the muck we sink into when we are compulsive debting so that we can be of service to others both in and out of program.

Just for Today: We can give all kinds of service within our Fellowship, but we start with our own solvency as the foundation.

December 10 — Selfishness

Before recovery, we not only wanted what we already had, but we wanted what you had too. When it came to sharing our resources, you could be sure that we'd be darned resentful if we thought we got the short end of the stick. In addition, we often felt an urgency to get what we wanted before anyone else got it because we were so afraid that there wouldn't be enough left. And sometimes there wasn't. When this happened, it was as if the world had come to an end. Now, that may sound extreme, but if we are honest, most of us surely experienced those feelings to a greater or lesser degree.

What a relief it is to live in recovery, where our perspective shifts to what we can give rather than what we can get. It's so much less stressful to willingly share our last cookie with love than hoard it for ourselves with fear that someone will take it from us. When we look through the lens of giving rather than getting, we can truly relax. But in order to receive this gift, we must first experience some degree of acceptance and the release of grasping that comes with working a program of recovery.

Just for Today: Start your day with a conscious effort to think of others first, treating them with kindness, respect, and compassion.

December 11   Sober in Business

It can be challenging for business owners who are personally solvent to walk the path of recovery with their business as well. Product-centered companies or those with employees may experience cash flow problems that can keep owners in a perpetual relapse. But when we are committed to running a sober business, we apply the same steps and principles as we do to our personal finances. For one thing, we do not turn to debt as our first option, but we do our best to ensure that any debt we take on is secured. It is accepted in D.A. that having something on the line (like a mortgage) is vastly different from the devil may care approach we compulsive debtors take with unsecured debting. We do our best to reinvest into the business rather than spending all our profit. We have a solid business and marketing plan to help us judiciously allocate our funds on spending that will make our business more profitable rather than just feeding the beast of our addiction. For those who are just starting out, especially solopreneurs, such as artists, writers, and consultants, we learn not to invest more than we can afford to start up our business.

Just for Today: If you want to start or run a solvent business, remember that the same rules apply to our business as to our personal recovery from compulsive debting and spending.

December 12 — Shame

Shame is a corrosive thread among us that has no place in recovery. The Merriam Webster Online Dictionary defines shame as "a feeling of guilt, regret, or sadness that you have because you know you have done something wrong." As we recover from the hopeless state of mind and body that is compulsive debting and spending, we are promised, on page 83 of the Big Book that we will "not regret the past nor wish to shut the door on it." We may have low credit scores or bills long past due. Our houses may have been foreclosed on or our cars repossessed. But as we clean up the wreckage of the past, we come to gain increased self-esteem, recognizing that our addiction doesn't define us. We acknowledge our past errors, but live in the present, doing our best not to let shame keep us from gaining material benefits we are due. A recovering D.A. member once paid over $1,000 more for car insurance annually because she was too ashamed to let the agent check her credit score. A few years later, she gained the courage to speak up … and received the reduced rate. In recovery, we learn that the judgment of others is not our business and that we have every right to strive for the same benefits as anyone else.

Just for Today: We will not let a feeling of shame drive our actions in recovery.

December 13 — Restraint

When we are upset, angry, or afraid, the tool of writing is suggested as a way to express our thoughts and feelings. But what happens next? Do we impulsively pick up the phone or press the Send button venting our spleen on the recipient of our displeasure? In recovery, we wait a day or more before making an impulse purchase to give us time to think more clearly about whether our decision is sober. So, too, we pause for at least 24 hours to see how our mind processes our emotions before taking action in highly charged situations. Once the dust settles, we are better able to sort through our feelings. How often have we been up in arms, self-righteously indignant and then 24 hours later had a completely different perspective? In many cases just the simple act of writing and rewriting, shared with our sponsor and network, provides us with the healing we seek. Sometimes, it is appropriate to take matters further, and sometimes, we realize that nothing good will come from doing so. Either way, there is nothing to lose by waiting, and a great deal of emotional sobriety to be gained. The rush to condemn feels similar to the pounding desire of obsession to buy, both of which are fueled by an excess of adrenaline coursing through our veins.

Just for Today: Using "restraint of tongue and pen" is a sure way to live without regret.

December 14 — Avoiding Pain

Addicts are expert at avoiding pain and maximizing pleasure. Or so they think. What they really do is play ping pong between them. Addicts in denial don't realize that using doesn't solve a problem; it just adds an additional layer on to it. No matter how high the momentary pleasure, it is always short-lived, and followed by long-term self-loathing and the wreckage we leave in our wake. We haven't actually avoided anything. In fact, the original problem has probably escalated while we were attempting to amuse ourselves by jumping off a cliff instead of dealing with the issue at hand.

It is ironic that addicts often use just when things are at their worst. We pull out the credit cards and go on a whirlwind spending binge just after being laid off. Or we order that big screen TV when we can't pay our rent. In recovery, we learn that pain is inevitable, but suffering is optional. By our willingness to accept the pain instead of running every which way to avoid it, we are able to come through the other side whole.

Just for Today: Do I believe that the momentary pleasure of compulsive debting and spending is not worth the world of pain and hurt that follows?

December 15   Holiday Gift Pressure

December is a month filled with gift giving. For recovering debtors and spenders, it is a challenging time. We must balance our desire to be generous on the one hand, with our available funds on the other. We may also have feelings of guilt, resentment, loneliness, or sadness thrown into the mix. A well-defined spending plan is the best weapon we have against the pressures of the season. If we are lucky, we have had an entire year to accumulate funds. But even if we are new to recovery, all we need is the willingness to live within our means, and let our sponsor, network, and PRG team help us fund our gift category in a reasonable, balanced way. Some of us will experience short-term growing pains our first season. But if we stay the course, we will come to respect our limits without feeling shame that we can't give more. Through this process, we may uncover previously untapped creativity, and happily discover that our homemade gift touched the recipient far deeper than any store bought item. If children complain or seem disappointed because they feel entitled to the level of extravagance that was part of our active addiction, we use the opportunity to teach them about financial responsibility, a gift that money can't buy.

Just for Today: Consider adding a homemade gift or heartfelt letter to the presents you give this year.

December 16 — The Mind

The mind is like a magician pulling rabbits out of hats. One minute, we could be furious with someone. The next, we might be laughing ourselves silly over the antics of our child or pet. Or we might experience a highly upsetting incident, yet the next morning, wake up to sunshine and birdsong feeling happy … until the memory of the day before floods in, ruining our good mood and setting us back into pain, anger, fear, or sadness. But even then, as we go through our day whole minutes or even hours might pass without any feeling or thought of what happened because we are fully present in whatever else we might be doing. This being the case, it is clear that, left to its own devices, the mind will conjure up all manner of thoughts that can bring us joy or sorrow. In recovery, we learn that we are not slaves to our mind, any more than we are slaves to our addiction. While we cannot keep a thought from seeping into our consciousness, we most certainly have the power of choice about what to do once it's there. We can nurse it, like a drink, or we can sweep it away, consciously bringing in more healing thoughts, a highly effective way to work Steps 6 and 7.

Just for Today: Just because the mind delivers up negative thoughts doesn't mean we have to ruminate on them.

December 17   Self-Care Is Vital

H.A.L.T. is an acronym in recovery circles, which stands for hungry, angry, lonely, or tired. Experiencing one or more of these conditions can lead us to poor decision-making around our spending. It's unrealistic to say we will never allow ourselves to overdo it, but we *can* remain mindful of the cumulative effect a lack of good self-care can have on us. Overdoing work or even enjoyable activities without taking a break creates an unbalanced life. Living on the edge is not conducive to serenity or sobriety. So, whether it's a work project, video game, craft, or sports activity that has captured our attention, we strive to tear ourselves away periodically so that we can rest and nourish our minds and bodies. If we sit and stare at, or type on, a screen endlessly, we can set a timer to get up and walk around periodically. Conversely, if we are on the go nonstop, we can use that same timer to remind us to take a break and eat a meal. One of the best ways to nurture an attitude of good self-care is by creating a daily Step 11 practice of prayer and meditation, which enables us to recharge our batteries, giving our minds and bodies a real opportunity for deep relaxation.

Just for Today: Make balance between activity and rest your goal.

December 18   Kindness and Compassion

Kindness and compassion are both elements of living a life of service. Kindness is the desire to be helpful while compassion takes it further to include the ability to relate to the suffering of others on a personal level. In either case, we do our best to engage in acts of kindness and compassion without desire for reward or reciprocity, and persist even in the face of a negative reaction. For instance, we see trash littered on our elderly neighbor's lawn and we remove it. But instead of thanks, the neighbor accuses us of snooping around. If we can show compassion in the face of the slight instead of anger and resentment, we are truly growing by leaps and bounds in our ability to be of service to others.

If we give so that we can get something in return, and become angry if we don't, our kindness is really a form of self-seeking. But when we can be of service and exhibit compassion no matter the cost to our ego, then we see that the D.A. promises of serenity and a rich life filled with meaning and purpose have really come true in our lives.

Just for Today: Do a kind deed with no expectation of thanks or reward.

December 19 — Rounding

Rounding is the practice of increasing or decreasing numbers to the nearest 5. So, for instance, $1.03 would round up to $1.05, while $1.02 would round down to $1.00. While rounding is used for tax payments and estimates, as a daily practice for compulsive debtors and spenders it can lead to confusion, vagueness, and errors. Because banks work with precision, if we round our numbers when tracking our spending, it will be nearly impossible to reconcile our spending with our bank account. Some people feel that precise accounting is an onerous burden that makes solvency too difficult. But for those of us who have embraced reporting to the penny, we have found it takes much less time to close out each month's spending with far fewer errors, and we are always clear on exactly how much money we have and how much we still owe. The simple fact is that recovering from compulsive debting and spending requires a level of discipline that is not needed when recovering from other types of addiction. Half measures avail us nothing. If we don't have clarity with our numbers, then we cannot trust our spending plan to be accurate. And without an accurate spending plan, we are in far greater danger of debting.

Just for Today: Remember that precision is the best way to maintain clarity with our numbers.

December 20 — Primary Purpose

Along with the steps, traditions, and tools, D.A. has also formulated a *Primary Purpose Statement* (also called the *San Diego Statement*). It says, in part, "We come together for one reason: because we are compulsive debtors, and the only way to not debt, one day at a time, is by helping another debtor practice the Twelve Steps." Even if we enter the program without one penny in unsecured debt, and believe that our core problem is compulsive spending, underearning, cluttering, procrastination, and/or time debting, still, our D.A. commitment is to live free from obtaining goods and services now for which we will pay in the future and for which we have not provided collateral, one day at a time. This is not to diminish the severity of other issues, but to remind us that we must, above all, not incur new unsecured debt. Finally, we are urged to recognize that while "visions, prosperity, and abundance are all wonderful side benefits of not debting," they are "not our primary purpose." The statement closes by saying, "we must be united on one simple message: Don't debt. We believe if we can do that the Fellowship of Debtors Anonymous will prosper and grow."

Just for Today: Whatever our other issues, can we accept the idea that our primary purpose in D.A. is to refrain from compulsive debting?

December 21 — Vacation

Taking a break from our routine is a great way to recharge our batteries and gain a fresh perspective on our life. However, just as someone who must take medication daily wouldn't dream of leaving their pills behind, neither can we pretend that we don't need our daily dose of recovery. While we may not be able to work our program exactly as we do at home, we don't have to eliminate what we *can* do because of what we can't. If we can't attend our regular meetings, we can download recordings of D.A. speakers onto our phone or tablet before we leave. Cruises often have 12 step meetings on board, and phone or Skype meetings are available around the world. We can create a spending plan specifically for our trip so that we don't have to worry about overspending, and we can keep track of our numbers wherever we are, though more caution may be required because of currency differences if we leave the country. All it takes to return home from our vacation abstinently is a little pre-planning before we leave. Instead of feeling that our recovery program is an albatross around our neck, we can view the effort to stay sober with money on vacation as a gift from our Higher Power to keep our recovery sailing smoothly.

Just for Today: Are you willing to plan your recovery into your vacation?

December 22 — Working the Steps

While we use the D.A. tools to aid us in the practical aspects of working our program, we must practice the steps if we want to experience the long-term relief we are promised. Some of us apply ourselves diligently to working the tools, but procrastinate in moving forward with the steps. While we may glide along for a while, experiencing some relief by keeping our numbers and going to meetings, without the firm foundation working the steps gives us we are more likely to relapse when faced with challenging financial or emotional situations.

Without working the steps, our recovery is built on a budget and a social network, but lacking the power of true accountability and dependence on a Power greater than ourselves that comes from doing the rigorous spiritual work that is necessary for true, long-term recovery from this hopeless state of body and mind. Instead of a house built with brick and cement, our recovery is like a house of cards that could collapse under its own weight at any moment. When we completely give ourselves over to fully working our program instead of engaging in half measures, we will build a strong foundation and a house that can withstand any storm.

Just for Today: What step are you working on?

December 23 — Half Measures

If we feel that we aren't experiencing the promises of the program, we may want to examine how much effort we're expending to work it. Page 59 of the Big Book states, "half measures availed nothing." It doesn't say that we will have some success if we just dance around the edges of recovery; it says that we won't get anywhere at all unless we practice the entire program. This means that not only do we work the steps formally, but we continue to practice them daily by following the instructions contained in steps 10, 11, and 12, which incorporate all the key elements of the other nine. So every day, we work on improving our character defects, taking responsibility for our actions, developing a stronger relationship with a Power greater than ourselves, and being of service to others. In so doing, our lives become an orchestra of recovery and our Higher Power the conductor. While such a daily routine may sound overwhelming when we first begin this journey, the miracle is that as we work the steps, we gradually and seamlessly weave these elements into our lives. And then we are in much less danger of relapse and much more likely to reap the rewards of recovery.

Just for Today: Do you have both feet firmly planted in recovery?

December 24 — Breaking the Cycle

Some of us were taught strange lessons about money growing up. Maybe a parent bought us gifts instead of spending time with us or we were taken shopping when we were hurting in an effort to stop the pain. Either of these behaviors could lead us to believe that money, and what it can buy, equals love and will solve all our problems. So then we grew up into full-blown compulsive debtors and spenders, and because our addiction took up all our energy, attention, and time, we continued the cycle, either out of guilt or by just seamlessly flowing into the role of giver based on our experience. We tried to fill the hole in our soul with goods and services and thought that it would work with everyone else. But instead, we were digging a deep, aching hole in the hearts of those we love. But we can repair the damage by simply being present today. That's all it takes to break the cycle: spending time with those we love. And when we do, we can rest assured that we are healing wounds instead of putting a band-aid on them.

Just for Today: Let's remember that we show our love with presence, not presents.

December 25 — Benevolence

Today is a good day to think about all the kindness and generosity we've been shown throughout our lives. Negative emotions like to take center stage, so we may find ourselves preoccupied with what we lack and how we feel we've been mistreated. But the fact is the kindness of others has been integral to our very existence. From the store clerk smiling at us to the doctor who delivered us, we are the beneficiaries of millions of benevolent acts throughout our lives, some of which we'll never even know about, such as an electrician who put in extra effort to ensure the wiring in your home exceeded safety standards. Certainly, we're conscious when the kindness resolves a problem, such as being graced with the life-saving act of a bystander or even the extra efforts of a customer service representative to resolve a pressing issue. But a stranger holding the door open for us or a clerk saying "take care" after serving us doesn't get our adrenaline pumping so we don't internalize it. Yet it soothes us like a cool breeze on a hot day, most certainly improving the quality of our lives. Let's remember that it's the accumulation of these small tokens of respect and graciousness given to each other that comprise the best of humanity.

Just for Today: Become gratefully conscious of each small act of kindness you are shown today.

December 26 — Pay It Forward

When we accept the generosity of others, whether in the form of money, goods, or services, they don't expect to be repaid. Most people give because it feels good. Despite that, we may feel uncomfortable with accepting gifts because even if the benefactor assures us that there are no strings attached, we may impose our own.

In recovery, we can shift our perspective on this issue. The philosophy of paying it forward means essentially that I do something nice for you and then you do something nice for someone else. Paying it forward is a humbling practice that can bring joy to our lives while giving us the opportunity to generously be of service.

The more we give to others, the better we feel about ourselves. As we make paying it forward a habit in our lives, we will find it easier to accept gifts and other acts of generosity without feeling guilty that we cannot reciprocate in kind.

Just for Today: Set in motion the cycle of paying it forward by committing an act of generosity with no expectation of receiving anything in return.

December 27   Comfort Spending

In the past, we may have gone on spending binges to make ourselves feel better when we were upset. The problem was that the good feeling didn't last and we were left with bills that we couldn't afford, items we didn't need, and a big dose of panic and remorse. There is just no way around facing discomfort if you are committed to living life on life's terms without drugging yourself in an attempt to avoid it. If our objective is to abstain from compulsive debting and spending, and if we believe that the 12 Steps are the way to recover from this hopeless state of body and mind, then we become willing to meet pain without using. When we don't pick up our drug, we see that the situation, and our feelings, eventually pass, leaving us, and our recovery, stronger. The program gives us "medicine" to mitigate our suffering without avoiding the pain, in the forms of literature to instruct us, a network to support us, and a Higher Power to carry us through. When we feel we are at our breaking point, we turn to our network to remind us of all we will lose by giving in to compulsive debting and spending, and we pray to our Higher Power, asking for the courage to stay sober with money until the feelings pass.

Just for Today: Can you see that using your drug will not bring you lasting comfort?

December 28   Retain, Return, or Regift?

At any time, but particularly during the holiday season, we may receive gifts that aren't to our liking. What to do about this is a quandary for everyone, but for compulsive debtors and spenders, the emotions around such a situation may be more highly charged. For instance, if we expected something better, we may find ourselves hell bent on buying what we really wanted to make up for our disappointment. Obsession and compulsion may be triggered in any case when we consider returning the item and deciding what else to buy. Or we may feel guilty about returning or re-gifting, worrying that the giver will expect to see us wearing or displaying their present. But whatever choice we make, the important thing is that we do our best to be right-minded about our decision and examine our thinking in light of our program to keep from acting impulsively. If we tend toward accumulation, perhaps the best choice for our recovery may be to donate or give the gift to someone else. But if we choose to return the item and buy something else, it's ok for us to enjoy whatever we select in its place. And if we end up keeping it, we can remind ourselves of the reason for the gift instead of focusing on what we dislike about it.

Just for Today: Try to appreciate the good intentions of the giver even if you don't like the gift.

December 29 — Choices

You may find that there isn't enough money for all your categories. But a closer look may show you that if you make different choices, you will have enough. But it may mean delaying gratification for what you want, or possibly choosing to spend less money on one or more discretionary activity. You may choose to buy one fewer pair of shoes or eat out less often if you want more money for clothes.

Money is finite. Yes, there is an infinite source, but the amount you have at any one moment is finite. You can wish and vision and pray all you want, but to my knowledge no one has ever made $1 equal $2. The key here is NOT to try to do this on your own. That is the purpose of the Pressure Relief Group (PRG), where two other D.A. members spend time with you (either in person or on the phone) to help you figure all this out.

Many of us have felt hopeless at times about how we will make our spending plan work. But with the help of our PRG, sponsor, and network, it always does.

Just for Today: Accept that being in recovery around money means making choices.

December 30   Deposits and Withdrawals

It is suggested that we pray, meditate, take inventory, contact other recovering debtors, and engage in service daily. Making the effort to establish this practice when times are easy will make it more likely that we will continue to engage in it, and find the relief it brings, when times are tough. The problem is that when times are easy, we get complacent and don't feel like making the effort. But when times are tough, beginning such a practice is nearly impossible. Consider this process akin to using a bank account. When we integrate recovery tools into our lives, we are making deposits. As we continue to practice each day, our "balance" builds up and our spiritual abundance increases. But when times get tough, we start making withdrawals. If we have not taken the time to establish a solid daily practice, we are no longer making deposits. Eventually, our account becomes overdrawn, and we risk relapse. The benefits of establishing our practice now are numerous: Meditation helps us become conscious of rumination rather than a slave to it. Having a network keeps us from isolating. Prayer offers us hope. Taking inventory keeps us right-minded. And giving service infuses our lives with purpose.

Just for Today: Try not to let complacency keep you from preparing for the tough times.

December 31 — Celebration

Many people celebrate New Year's Eve with parties, excess, and over-indulgence, promising to stop compulsive debting and spending tomorrow. But there is no reason why we can't enjoy New Year's Eve while living within our means. We can also use this once-a-year occasion to take stock of where we are on our path and celebrate our progress.

Today is a perfect day to begin or continue a commitment to abstinence from compulsive debting and spending. The Big Book promises that "we will not regret the past nor wish to shut the door on it." We can reflect on the year that has passed and acknowledge mistakes we may have made over the past twelve months. But we can also celebrate our progress in recovery.

D.A.'s first promise is that once we commit to recovery, "where once we felt despair, we will experience a newfound hope." Yes, another year is ending. But today is a day of hope if we are willing to be sober with money now. Tomorrow, the New Year begins. But we don't have to wait until then to begin our recovery.

Just for Today: It's never too soon to recover.

Resources

Debtors Anonymous
DebtorsAnonymous.org

Debtors Anonymous Telephone Intergroup
DATIG.org

Underearners Anonymous
underearnersanonymous.org

The blog on which this book is based:
Getting Out from Going Under: A Guide to Recovery for Compulsive Debtors and Spenders
Gettingoutfromgoingunder.wordpress.com

"I Can't Stop Spending!" Podcast
Download the 54 episodes of the "I Can't Stop Spending!" Podcast.
Icantstopspending.wordpress.com

For help with creating a spending plan,
sign up for the FREE
Fearless Budgeting course
FearlessBudgeting.wordpress.com

About the Author

Susan B. first came into Debtors Anonymous in 1999 and paid off over $22,000 of unsecured debt. Thinking she had the answer, she left the program.

After a six year relapse, Susan finally hit bottom. When she came out of the fog in the spring of 2009, she realized that she'd now accrued over $34,000 in credit card debt and couldn't afford to pay for her son to begin college in the fall.

On April 25, 2009, she cut up her credit cards and recommitted herself to Debtors Anonymous. Working her recovery program, she began using the ideas in this book to keep from debting and out-of-control spending one day at a time.

Through the miracle of the program, Susan's son was able to start college in the fall of 2009 and he graduated in 2013. Despite becoming disabled in 2010, which severely reduced her income, Susan finished paying off her debt in 2015 and has continued staying abstinent one day at a time with the help and the Grace of her Higher Power.

***

Susan is also an artist, and writes about chronic illness, emotional sobriety, recovery from compulsive overeating, and creativity challenges. Find out more at HealingDoodle.com.

Printed in Great Britain
by Amazon